CAREERS, COMPACTS & DISCOS

Also by Anne Dart Taylor

True God's Priest

A biography of my father, The Rev'd Thomas Henry Dart

Published by Memoir Club 2008

ISBN 978-1-84104-182-7

Malawi Memories

An Account of life in Malawi 1967-1971, taken from letters

Published by Vale Press Ltd 2012

ISBN 980-0-9564156-2-2

Errata:

For Pat Smith read Pat White:

pp 118, 157; 194; 208; 243.

CAREERS, COMPACTS & DISCOS

How Education and Industry worked together in the Inner London Education Authority 1982-1990

By

ANNE DART TAYLOR

All rights reserved.

No part of this publication may be published
or transmitted in any form or by any means
without permission from the publisher.

© Anne Dart Taylor 2015

ISBN-13: 978-1517171070

ISBN-10: 1517171075

PROLOGUE

When the Inner London Education Authority (ILEA) was set up in 1965, Anne Dart Taylor was teaching history in a girls' grammar school in Maida Vale. By the time the ILEA was disbanded by the Conservative Government in 1990, she was Staff Inspector for Careers Education and Guidance and Schools Industry Links, heading up three teams of Advisory Teachers, Divisional Industry Schools Co-ordinators, (DISCOS) and work experience co-ordinators.

Not all the years in between were spent in London. In 1967, Anne and her husband went to Malawi, where she taught in African secondary schools. They returned to London in 1974. In 1978, when both her daughters were at middle school, Anne took a job teaching in Merton, South London. It was a time of high youth unemployment, race riots and the introduction of YOPs and YTS. Concerned about the future of her pupils, Anne took on the newly created post of Head of Careers in 1980

She always hoped to return to the ILEA so, when she saw a post advertised for a 'divisional schools industry co-ordinator' (DISCO) in Camden & Westminster in 1982, she applied for it and was successful. She made contact with the other DISCOs, some of whom were members of the Schools Council Industry Project (SCIP), learning from their experience how to prepare pupils for the world of work by bringing schools, colleges and businesses together, through projects like Transition to Working Life (TWL); mini-enterprises, and teachers' secondment to industry.

In 1984, Anne was appointed to Catherine Avent's team of careers inspectors and given responsibility for the DISCOs, whose numbers were made up to 10, one for each ILEA Division. Initially, the most junior of three inspectors, the retirement of Cathy Avent, the Senior Inspector, six months later, and the tragic death of Cathy's successor, David Chambers in 1987, left Anne as Acting Staff Inspector, with the task of rebuilding the careers education and guidance team of inspectors and advisory teachers, using them to support the work of careers teachers in schools and colleges.

Sir William Stubbs, the Chief Education officer of the ILEA, asked Anne to take part in talks with a number of major firms, such as B.P. and Whitbread's, about setting up a Compact between schools and Industry in the East End of London, one of the most deprived areas of the country. The East London Compact was launched, in 1986 by HRH Prince Charles. Pupils in Compact Schools were given challenging targets to improve attendance and punctuality; complete their courses of study and a London Record of Achievement. In return they were offered work experience and potential priority hiring by local firms. Teachers were seconded to industry and business people came into schools, shadowing teachers and heads to get a better understanding of education. The DISCOs and work-experience co-ordinators were the key facilitators. Within a short time, 50 other Compacts were set up in other deprived areas in London and around the country.

Despite the success of the Compacts, the Conservative Government disbanded the ILEA in 1989, giving the 12 London Boroughs responsibility for education. Anne applied to Camden, where she had worked as a DISCO, and was appointed as a Senior Inspector for Student Learning and Assessment.

ABOUT THE AUTHOR

Anne Dart Taylor

Anne was educated at King Edward VI's High School, Birmingham, the Oxford High School and St Hilda's College, Oxford, where she read history. After two years as a reporter and sub-editor on the *Church Times*, she decided to go into teaching. Her first post was in Paddington & Maida Vale High School, in the Inner London Education Authority (ILEA).

In 1965, she married the Rev'd Humphrey Taylor, then a curate in Notting Hill. Their first daughter, Katy, was born in 1966, just before Humphrey went out to Malawi to take up the post of Rector of Lilongwe. Their second daughter, Lizzie, was born in

Malawi in 1968. Anne taught history in two African Secondary Schools.

In 1971, when Humphrey was deported by Dr Banda, the family returned to England. Humphrey was appointed Chaplain to Bishop Grossteste College in Lincoln in 1972. Anne taught part time at Christ's Hospital School.

In 1974, Humphrey's next job as secretary for Chaplains in Higher Education, was based in London so the family moved to Wimbledon. Anne completed an MPhil in racism in history textbooks and returned to full time work, teaching history in a Merton School where she later took on the role of head of careers .

In 1982, Anne went back into the ILEA, as a divisional industry schools co-ordinator (DISCO). She became a careers inspector in 1984 and three years later, Staff Inspector for Careers Education and School Industry links. She was involved in setting up the East London Compact. When the ILEA was broken up, in 1989, Anne moved to London Borough of Camden as a Senior Inspector, for Student Learning and Assessment.

In 1990, Humphrey was consecrated Bishop of Selby, which entailed a move to York. For a term, Anne commuted weekly, between London and York, while serving out her notice with Camden. Anne was appointed Principal Inspector of Schools by the Metropolitan Borough of Doncaster, a post which she held for five years, from 1991-1996. During that time she trained as a Registered Inspector of Secondary Schools with OFSTED and with her team inspected a number of secondary schools outside

Doncaster itself. She was also President of the National Association of Careers and Guidance Teachers (NACGT).

She took early retirement in 1996, but continued to do OFSTED inspections and inspections of church schools, as well as running training courses for careers teachers and working on National Occupational Standards for Advice and Guidance. When Humphrey retired in 2003, he and Anne moved to a village in Worcestershire, where she continues her involvement in education as chair of governors of the village school.

Anne has written two other books: *True God's Priest,* a biography of her father, Tom Dart, and *Malawi Memories,* an account of the time she and Humphrey spent in Malawi.

Contents

PREFACE

The Inner London Education Authority 1965-1990

When the Inner London Education Authority (ILEA) was formed on 1 April 1965, I was teaching history in one of its schools. I had started working at Paddington and Maida Vale High School four years before, under the London County Council. I am not sure I even noticed the change, though I probably read about it in the ILEA newspaper. It made no difference to me, as long as my salary was paid into my bank account each month.

When the ILEA was abolished on 1st April 1990, I was Staff Inspector for Careers Education and Guidance and School-Industry links. ILEA's demise made a huge impact on me and I grieved over its dissolution. The teams I led, of careers inspectors, advisory teachers and divisional industry co-ordinators, were disbanded, among many others.

My time in the inspectorate happened to coincide with a critical period in the history of the ILEA. It was a wonderful Authority to work for, offering its teachers unparalleled in-service training in its innumerable teachers' centres, and access to up-to-the-minute information technology and multi-media, right across the curriculum. However, the ILEA had been criticised for becoming overly bureaucratic and complacent because of its wealth and influence in the capital city. It was also true that while there were many good or even excellent schools in the Authority, there were some which were failing.

Under the leadership of Chief Inspector Dr David Hargreaves, the role of the inspectorate changed. It was given a harder edge and used to tackle failing schools. We were now required to make regular, 'substantial visits' to individual departments within schools, based on the publication *Keeping the School Under Review.* Dr Hargreaves also instituted a rigorous programme of full school inspections. Collaborating with colleagues was a profound learning experience for me and one which was to stand me in good stead when I later became an OFSTED inspector.

Writing about that time has been like stirring a bowl of potpourri. I have caught again, from the dry pages of reports, speeches, newspaper articles and minutes of meetings, a faint aroma of the excitement, risk and tragedy of that period, when the Labour-led Authority was in mortal combat, political and educational, with the Conservative Government of Mrs. Thatcher.

At the beginning of the struggle, I was a mere foot soldier, but in a time of war, people have to act up to replace fallen comrades – this was literally true in my case. After the tragic death, in March 1987, of my colleague, David Chambers, I became Acting – later Substantive - Staff Inspector for Careers Education and School-Industry links and was involved in setting up the East London Compact between schools and businesses in London.

I was charged with building links between schools and industry in the ILEA, during the 13 year period from 1978-1991. Our crowning achievement was the development of the East London Compact, which brought together industry and education to offer better career opportunities to pupils in ILEA schools. Originally operating in Hackney and Tower Hamlets, Compacts spread first across all 10 Divisions of the ILEA and later across the country.

My teams of inspectors, careers advisory teachers and divisional industry schools co-ordinators (DISCOs) became enablers and training providers for other groups, for example those involved in the Technical and Vocational Education Initiative; the Certificate of Prevocational Education and the London Record of Achievement.

Ironically, though Compacts were rolled out across the country by the Thatcher Government, its hostility to the ILEA did not diminish. First, the Greater London Council was abolished in 1986 and the ILEA became a directly elected Education Authority. Then, in 1989, the ILEA itself was destroyed by Act of Parliament and replaced by 12 Inner London Boroughs in 1990.

The ILEA's legacy of links between education and industry continued for a while. The new education authorities, staffed for the most part by former ILEA heads, teachers and inspectors continued many of the ILEA's policies. Compacts, linking schools and business, continued to flourish, supported by the Technical and Vocational Education Initiative and the Certificate of Pre-Vocational Education. In addition, Compacts spread outside London across the country, until by 1990, there were 50 funded Compacts.

As Professor Andrew Miller [1] says, the period from 1988 to 1994 was significant for the involvement of three government departments, Education, Employment and Trade & Industry, supporting Education Business Partnerships (EBPs). 'The Partnership Initiative funded EBPs right across the country for the first time. It encouraged Training and Enterprise Councils to work with Local Education Authorities to set up local EBPs.' The Department for Trade and Industry funded both the Mini-Enterprise project in schools and teacher placements in industry via Understanding British Industry.

Inevitably, over time, that legacy became dissipated. By 1994, the Partnership and Education and Enterprise Initiatives had come to an end and TVEI funding was running out. 'Some national funding for EBPs was routed through the 82 Training and Enterprise Councils (e.g. for work experience from 1995) but there were wide variations in levels of funding.'[2] Without the money,

---

[1] Andrew Miller, *Literature Review*: QCA 2007 p 22
[2] Andrew Miller idem p 23

schools had little incentive to continue with the time consuming practice of setting up links with business, particularly when they were wrestling with the introduction of Kenneth Baker's National Curriculum in 1989, which signally omitted to mention careers education.

Twenty five years later, there is once again pressure on schools from a Conservative Government to implement a formal academic curriculum. Opportunities for work experience or work shadowing for 16 year old students are no longer provided as a matter of course by schools and internships for undergraduates are available only to the most privileged classes. Cruelly, the young people living on so-called 'Benefits Street', who need the most help, are the least likely to receive it and the most likely to face unemployment.

In 2015, however, there is a new twist. It is not merely the lowest social groups who are at risk. A *Guardian* [3] report suggests 'more people are moving down rather than up the social ladder as the number of middle-class managerial and professional jobs shrinks, according to an Oxford University study. The experience of upward mobility … has become less common in the past four decades... Dr John Goldthorpe, co-author of the study and an Oxford sociologist says "For the first time …we have a generation coming through education and into the jobs market whose chances

---

[3] Patrick Butler, The Guardian , 6.11.2014

of social advancement are not better than their parents, they are worse."

'The UK's boom in managerial and professional level public services and industrial jobs during the 1950s, 1960s and 1970s saw an increase in the number of children born into professional and managerial families. The decline in these jobs meant that the number of individuals at risk of downward mobility is significantly greater.'

Figures from the Office of National Statistics confirm this: 'The proportion of graduates working in non-graduate jobs has risen from 37% in April to June 2001 to 47% in April to June 2013... This may reflect a lower demand for graduate skills as well as an increased supply of graduates.'[4]

In a situation of downward social mobility, it is even more essential that schools should prepare young people of all abilities and all backgrounds for the transition to adult and working life so they can make informed choices. Many young people have unrealistic expectations, fostered by television programmes, of becoming 'a celebrity' but even those whose feet are firmly on the ground, make hundreds of job applications without success. Work experience, work simulations, mini enterprises and visits by employers to schools are not only useful for those planning to leave school at the earliest opportunity. Links between business

---

[4] Source: Office for National Statistics

and schools enrich the curriculum and enable all students to have an understanding of the world of work. They also foster better relationships between teachers and business people.

Of course, there are still pockets of good practice to be found up and down the country but these isolated examples need to be joined up into a more substantial network so that there is a universal entitlement for young people, not merely those who are already well connected. In writing this account, my intention has been to put on record the achievements of the ILEA and those who worked in it, in the hope that teachers and business people might be inspired to take up the baton and re-establish school-industry links in the twenty-first century.

* * *

When I first embarked on this project, I feared I might have to rely on memory alone but when I started searching the attic, I was amazed to discover how many of my own files had survived two major house moves, from London to York and from York to the Vale of Evesham. I have also been helped by several former colleagues, who searched their own memories and attics.

Organising this material into a coherent whole has been difficult, because so many different coloured threads were woven into the fabric of my job: in-service training for careers teachers, recruited from a variety of backgrounds; attendance at the appointments of heads of departments by governing bodies; appraisal of members of my teams; pastoral visits to schools; full inspections, called by the Chief Inspector; meetings with the Careers Service and with members of the London Education Business Partnership, which set up the first Compact between education and industry in East London.

I had to make a decision, whether to pull out each of these threads separately or to cut strips across the material, in which case there would be a lot of loose ends. I finally decided to arrange this account into thematic sections (strips), though each is written chronologically (following the threads). In real life, of course, many of the events I describe overlapped or ran alongside each other.

CHAPTER ONE

The Birth of the Inner London Education Authority 1963

In 1963, the London Government Act created the Inner London Education Authority (ILEA) to take over the educational responsibilities of the London County Council.[5] Originally this was a provisional move but its status was made permanent in 1965. Technically, the Greater London Council (GLC) was the education authority for Inner London. However, to avoid outer London Boroughs having an input to Inner London schools, which were no concern of theirs, the GLC delegated responsibility to the ILEA as a 'special committee'. In 1985, the ILEA was reconstituted by the Local Government Act, as a directly elected, stand-alone body.

My first contact with schools in London happened in 1961. After leaving Oxford I had worked as a reporter and sub-editor on the *Church Times,* in Portugal Street, for 18 months. Just at the time when I was hoping to move to a bigger paper, the *News Chronicle* folded and I found myself competing for jobs with much more experienced journalists.

---

[5] The Outer London Boroughs such as Merton, became Local Education Authorities in their own right

I took a job as a supply teacher in Plumstead School for a term. I enjoyed it sufficiently to apply for a permanent post, teaching history at Paddington and Maida Vale High School (PMVHS) in September 1961 and was offered the position, largely on the recommendation of the Head at Plumstead. I had no teaching qualification, but I did have an Oxford degree in history and, once I had passed my probationary year, I was recognised as a qualified teacher by the Department for Education and Science.

PMVHS was founded by Henrietta Barnett, who donated some stained glass windows to the library. The school had been part of the Girls' Public Day School Trust for a while, but was taken over first by the LCC and then the ILEA. [6]

Numbers of Jewish refugees from the Holocaust settled in the Maida Vale area, before and after the Second World War and their daughters came to PMVHS. We also had three Jewish members of staff and eventually a Jewish head. The staff room was an unusually happy place and members of it still meet, half a century later. The only cause of dissension was between those who smoked (of whom, regrettably, I was one) and those who didn't. The local Rabbi came into the school to give the Jewish girls religious instruction. In the winter, they were allowed to go home early, before it became dark, on Fridays.

---

[6] Sadly, the school no longer exists. The building was taken over by Paddington College of FE.

Assemblies were interesting. They began with an Anglican service led by the Head, Miss Spong. [7] Staff and pupils knelt on the bare floorboards for prayers. The Jewish girls then joined us and a psalm was recited, omitting the Christian doxology. When that was over, the Roman Catholics came in, having had their own service in a classroom. Then notices were given out.

I was second in the History department. The head of department, Miss Whitlock, was a formidable person. I believe her fiancé had been killed in the First World War. In addition to history, I also taught English and R.E. and was a form tutor. Despite the age of the building and the fact that classrooms were often separated from each other only by folding screens, I loved teaching there.

Towards the end of my time at PMVHS, I was charged with organising trips out of school for fifth formers at the end of the summer term. Most of them had never been outside Maida Vale. I took them to the Houses of Parliament and Westminster Abbey – as one girl confessed, 'I thought it was a cemetery, Miss, because so many people were buried there.' With Dr Lusty, who replaced Miss Whitlock as Head of department, I took them to the Royal Academy. The girls and I arrived there safely but Dr Lusty got lost *en route*.

---

[7] When Miss Spong retired she was succeeded by Miss Gepstein, who was Jewish. She also came into assembly for the psalms.

I left PMVHS in 1966. By that time I was married to Humphrey Taylor and was expecting our first child. We were also planning to go Malawi. Humphrey had been appointed Rector of St Peter's Lilongwe, and during our five years in Malawi I taught history[8] in two African Secondary Schools.

---

[8] Despite the fact that Malawi had become independent, students for the Cambridge exam (O level equivalent) , studied Empire and Commonwealth History in 30 year old textbooks. This was later replaced by the history of Central and Southern Africa.

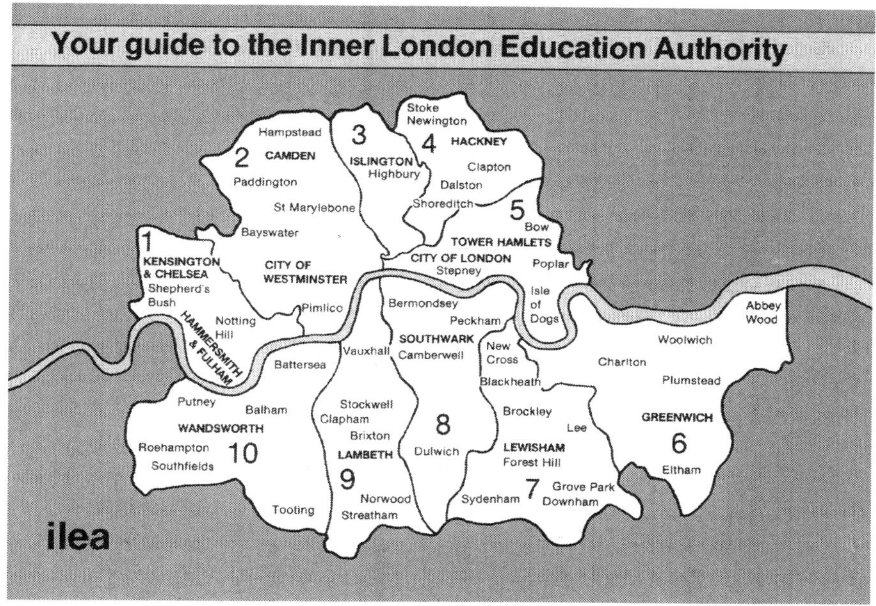

ILEA Divisions

CHAPTER TWO

Back to London 1978-80

It was 1974 before we returned to London. Humphrey had been newly appointed by the Church of England Board of Education as secretary for chaplains in Higher Education. His office was in Church House, in Westminster. I wanted to live in Notting Hill, where we had a flat when we were first married, but we couldn't afford a house with a garden in what was a rapidly gentrifying neighbourhood. The number of yellow front doors was increasing by leaps and bounds.

Friends from Malawi, John and Alison Leake, had bought a house in Wimbledon and told us there were good schools there. We stayed with them while we were house-hunting and bought an Edwardian semi-detached house in Raynes Park. Our daughters, aged 8 and 6, went to the local primary school, in the London Borough of Merton.

Though house prices were nothing like they are today, our mortgage ate up a substantial portion of Humphrey's salary. I was finishing my M. Phil., on racism in history textbooks, and did some part time teaching in Merton schools. In 1978, when our daughters were 12 and 10, I started looking for a full-time job. I found plenty of vacancies in *The Times Educational Supplement* but for most of them, I was judged to be too experienced, too highly qualified and therefore too expensive.

Eventually, I found a job covering a maternity leave, not in the ILEA, as I'd hoped, but in the Outer London Borough of Merton. I started teaching at Willows High School in September1978. After two terms the job became permanent.

Willows High School, despite its name, was a comprehensive. As a result of the Labour Party's education policy, introduced by Tony Crosland in 1965, an amalgamation had taken place between a girls' grammar school and a girls' secondary modern. They had been housed in separate buildings on the same site, so the amalgamation ought not to have been too traumatic. However, when I worked there, 10 years later, the teachers from the two schools were still sitting on opposite sides of the one staff room, not talking to each other.

This was my first full-time job in a comprehensive school. The girls I taught in PMVHS in London and Christ's Hospital, Lincoln, where we lived on returning from Malawi, had been well behaved and the Malawian boys and girls were desperate for the education their parents struggled to pay for. For the first term, at Willows, I had difficulty in establishing control in some forms. My task was made harder because I taught in a mobile classroom at the front of the school, which was *en route* to the playing fields. Girls going to P.E. made faces though the windows. However, by my second term, I had found the knack of managing my classes and grew in confidence as a result.

Once, in my third year at Willows, I was sitting in my empty classroom, marking books during a free period, when a new teacher came past, in floods of tears, because the girls in her class were rioting. She went off to tell the deputy head. I wrestled with my conscience. Should I go down the corridor and attempt to calm the girls down? What if they did some damage to the furniture or building? Or hurt someone? Was it my responsibility? I decided it was.

When I walked into the room, the girls were standing on the desks and window sills, cheering because they had won. As I had guessed, they were the girls who had given me trouble in my first term but with whom I had now established good relations.

I sat down at the teacher's desk, in silence, and folded my hands to prevent them from shaking.

They shouted gleefully: 'We've been very bad, Miss.'

I made no response.

This unnerved them. Their euphoria collapsed like a pricked balloon. One by one, they climbed down and sat in their places. When all was quiet, I told them they had been unkind to their teacher and I was disappointed in them. I asked what work they had been doing. They muttered that they had been reading *Jane Eyre*.

'Right,' I said. 'Open your books and we will carry on from

where you left off.'

They picked up their books from the floor and window ledges where they had been thrown.

'Can I read first, Miss?' asked the ring leader.

I said yes. By the time the deputy head arrived, breathing fire and smoke, the girls were calmly taking it in turns to read aloud. She seemed dumb founded but I handed the class over to her and returned to marking exercise books. Later she said to me:

'You will never make a head, Anne, until you enjoy shouting at pupils.'

I thought, but did not say: 'In that case I don't want to be a head.'

*　　　*　　　*

The pupils at Willows High School came from a variety of social classes and races. The white girls were in a majority but were divided into those whose middle class parents expected their daughters to stay on into the sixth form, and those whose working class parents encouraged them to leave school at the earliest opportunity.

Of course there were exceptions, like the daughter of the school caretaker, a card-carrying communist, who was one of my brightest A level students and went on to university. She was afraid that A level examiners might mark her down because of her political views but I assured her that, provided her essays were factually correct and her arguments logical, the examiners would not penalise her. On the contrary, I told her, they might be relieved to read something out of the ordinary. I am glad to say I was right

Willows also had a small group of aspirational East African Asians, refugees from Malawi and Uganda, who were bullied by the English girls. There were also a few Black British, who travelled from Brixton, courtesy of the Northern Line. One of them, Maureen, was in my tutor group, which was a vertical one, including pupils from each year. Maureen stayed with me for the whole of her time in the school, becoming my prefect.

In the third, fourth and fifth years, [9] there were two streams, one sitting the Ordinary Level General Certificate of Education (GCE) in British 19th & 20th century political history and the other taking the Certificate of Secondary Education (CSE) which focussed on the Industrial Revolution in Britain in the 18th and 19th centuries. Having taught African history in Malawi, I was acutely aware how Eurocentric these syllabuses, chosen by the head of department, were.

With the support of the excellent local authority adviser, Eileen Harries, I persuaded the head of department to change the syllabus to include more world history. I was not alone in this. There was, in Merton, a local group of teachers of world history, which I convened. I was also a member of the political science group and vice chair of the education panel of the Community

---

[9] Years 8,9, and 10 in today's terminology

Relations Council.

The ILEA generously opened its courses to teachers from the outer London boroughs. Occasionally, I had the opportunity to go to lectures on the teaching of history run at the ILEA's History and Social Sciences Teachers' Centre in Clapham, which was accessible by underground or car. I envied the wealth of resources held at the centre and wistfully hoped I might one day work in the ILEA again.

The girls in the O level classes in Willows, were bright and hard-working, like the grammar school pupils I had taught previously. Some went on to further education colleges but several stayed on in the sixth form to do their A levels and a few planned to go on to university. Several girls in the CSE sets also worked hard to convert their results into O level equivalents by gaining a Grade 1, but I was distressed to discover a disaffected group of girls who had no higher ambition than to quit school at the earliest opportunity and have a baby.

Given the high levels of youth unemployment, this perhaps was not unexpected. Having a baby seemed to them a positive career choice. The pregnant girls hoped the local council would give them a flat where they could live with their new-born child. More often they remained with their parents or, at best, ended up in bed-and-breakfast accommodation.

James Callaghan introduced the Youth Opportunity Scheme (YOP), in 1978, which offered young people work experience on employers' premises known, somewhat unfortunately, as 'WEEP'. Some of the placements were of poor quality, as were the training opportunities. Despite this, 162,000 young people took YOP up in 1978-9 and 550,000 in 1981-2.

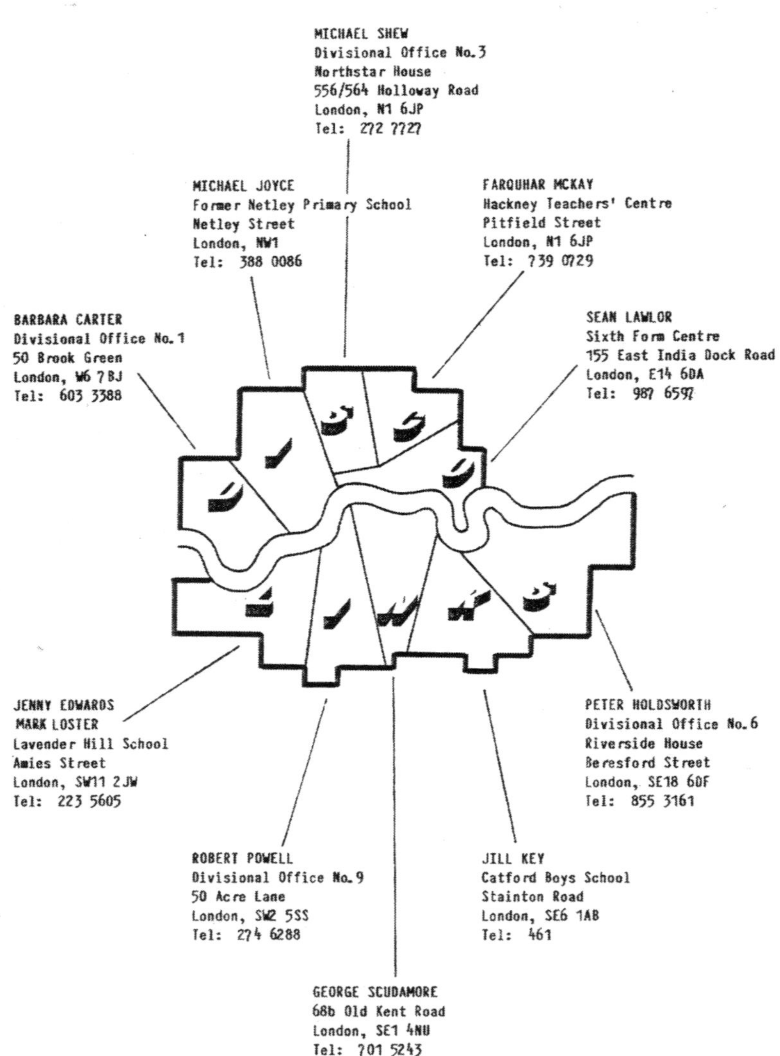

DISCOs in 1982

CHAPTER THREE

Head of Careers 1980-1982

In April 1979, Margaret Thatcher became Prime Minister for the first time. Her manifesto 'proclaimed a philosophy of business and free enterprise and promised, by implication, a painful shake-out of subsidised jobs in ailing firms.'[10] However, she did not set out in detail what this would mean. The campaign 'talked about lower taxes but not about higher unemployment. It vowed that public spending would be cut but there wasn't a word about cutting public services.'[11]

By the second half of 1980, 'unemployment was up by more than 800,000 and hundreds of manufacturing businesses were going bust, throttled by the rising exchange rate. Prices were up 22% in a year, wages by a fifth. At the Tory Conference of 1980, cabinet dissidents began to make speeches, subtly criticizing the whole project These were dismissed by Thatcher: "You turn if you

---

[10] Hugo Young; *One of Us*; Pan Books, 1990; p129
[11] Idem p139

want to, the lady's not for turning."[12]

I worried about the future prospects of many of my students. Unfortunately, in the early 1980s a large cohort of young people reached the age of 16 'at a time when unemployment reached post war high levels with calamitous implications for the employment of school leavers.'[13]

It was against this political and economic background that I decided to apply for the post of careers teacher in Willows, when it became vacant in 1980. The lack of careers education in the school had been severely criticised in a General Inspection and the careers teacher had resigned. A new Scale 3 post was created for Head of Careers.

The only other applicant for the job was the business studies teacher who had been in the school for a while. I had no experience at all but I did my homework, going to the Ursuline Convent School in Wimbledon to talk to the careers teacher there, Oonagh Linehan, who lent me a book, entitled *Practical Approaches to Careers Education (PACE)*[14]. It was written by Catherine Avent, Senior Inspector for Careers Education in the Inner London Education Authority (ILEA.) I devoured it, from the

---

[12] Andrew Marr: A History of Modern Britain, first published by Macmillan 2007; in paperback by Pan 2008 p 388

[13] P. Dolton, F. Galinda-Rueda & G. Makepeace, *The Long Term Effect of Government Sponsored Training* ; version 1 p1; Newcastle University, Centre for Economic Performance, (LSE) , Cardiff University, July 2004

[14] Third edition, 1978; Hobsons Press (Cambridge) Ltd.

first page to the last. On the basis of that, I got the job.

From my predecessor, I inherited a locked filing cabinet, kept in an inaccessible room on the top floor of the school. When I finally forced the cabinet open, I discovered it contained a kettle and a number of out of date leaflets, which I threw in the bin. I joined the National Association of Careers and Guidance Teachers (NACGT), and studied their Journal, which gave me information about materials and ideas for lessons. I also enrolled on a two year diploma course in careers education and guidance at Southlands College. The course and the people I met there gave me the knowledge and courage to tackle my new post.

One of the first speakers, Cathy Avent, herself, was inspirational. Cathy was a brilliant raconteur, making us laugh with her stories, while she inculcated the value and necessity of good careers education. She had served in the Women's Royal Navy Service during the Second World War, was educated at Lady Margaret Hall, Oxford and the LSE. She had worked for 18 years in the London Careers Service before being appointed the first Inspector for Careers Education and Guidance in the ILEA in 1964.

*   *   *

My head was buzzing with ideas about my new job. I asked Miss Elkin, the head of Willows, if I could move out of the mobile classroom to a large hall in the lower building, which became part class room and part careers room, to which the pupils had open access.

Once the assembly hall in the secondary modern school, it had been the home base for Neptune, one of the four houses in Willows. The head of Neptune never forgave me for turning her out[15] but I found the space invaluable. I could stock careers materials on open shelves, instead of in a filing cabinet, and put up posters round the walls.

It was equally useful for the history lessons, which I was still teaching full time. At last, my pupils had space to re-enact historical scenes and to make and display models of castles and houses. My history colleague, Denise Jardine, and I completed a course, which qualified us as 'sub-standard cinema projectionists'.

Our certificates of competence caused much laughter. Denise and I had to explain that we had passed the course with flying colours and were competent projectionists, it was the projector which was smaller than those used in cinemas and therefore classified as 'sub-standard.' The qualification enabled us to show 16 mm history filmstrips. Denise brought her classes into my room so they could watch as well.

In my second year, my history timetable was reduced so that I was able to organise a programme of careers education throughout the 13-18 school. Miss Elkin timetabled careers lessons, by putting them on a carousel with mathematics, which

---

[15] House meetings had to be held in one of the science labs.

was naturally unpopular with the mathematics staff but delighted the pupils. Every time they passed me in the corridor they asked me: 'Is it our turn for careers this week?'

Third years had a careers lesson once every three weeks, to help them with their subject options, by developing self-knowledge and decision-making skills and giving them information about careers. Fourth years had a weekly lesson, taught by a team of teachers, who volunteered to assist me. I provided games, simulations and questionnaires to help the girls to work in groups, as well as on their own, and to make more realistic job choices.

Once I took over the careers role, my relationship with the pupils changed radically. I believed it had been good before, but now girls approached me to have private conversations about their future. I rarely got to the staff room at break, because I was so often waylaid. Sometimes I had to make difficult choices between my loyalty to the school and my duty as a careers adviser. For example, one bright Asian girl asked whether she should stay in the sixth form or go to Kingston College to do science A levels. I rang the college to check on numbers taking science A levels and what the outcomes were. The college had classes of 16+ as against three in the school and their results were better. I passed on the information to her so she could make her own choice.

*　　*　　*

I began to organise visits for the girls to workplaces, outside the school, and invited speakers from industry to come in. My 1982 diary records the dates when Miss M. Bellars gave a talk about journalism; Mrs Atkinson spoke about careers in fashion and Mr Connolly, described the hairdressing course at Kingston College of Further Education.

The programme was arranged with difficulty because I had no telephone of my own.[16] I had to go to the school office and ask the secretary if I could use hers, so it was essential to keep on the right side of her. I also had to negotiate with the helpful laboratory assistants in the science block, where the television was based. I worked out a rota with them which enabled my classes to watch the excellent BBC careers programmes. I was rapidly discovering that careers teachers needed to develop powers of persuasion and, when necessary, to beg, borrow and even steal the tools of their trade, to give their pupils the best possible life chances at a time when the economic situation continued to be dire.

The folly of leaving large numbers of unskilled young unemployed to find their own solutions was underlined by rioting, just across the border from Merton, in Lambeth, where some of Willows' pupils, including Maureen, lived.

> 'In early April 1981 riots broke out in Brixton, shops were burned and looted, streets barricaded and more than 200 people, most of them police, were injured...Lord Scarman was asked to hold a public inquiry; but in the first week of

[16] There were of course no mobiles at that time, just landlines.

July trouble began again, this time in the heavily Asian west London suburb of Southall, with petrol bombs, arson attacks and widespread pelting of the police.'[17]

[17] Andrew Marr: idem p389

CHAPTER FOUR

Divisional Industry Schools Co-ordinator 1982-4

I had been doing the job of careers co-ordinator in Willows for two years when at Easter 1982, I saw an advertisement in the *Times Educational Supplement* for two jobs as 'Divisional Industry Schools Co-ordinators (DISCOs)' in the Inner London Education Authority (ILEA). They were Scale 4 posts, working to Cathy Avent, OBE. I decided to apply for one of them.

When I asked Miss Elkin for a reference, she immediately offered me the position of head of history as well as head of careers on a Scale 4, if I stayed in the school. I was torn, because I loved teaching history and had often been frustrated by the lack of support and resources from my elderly head of department, who kept everything locked up in her cupboard. I felt like weeping, when I eventually saw the pristine volumes stockpiled there.

However, the DISCO job was even more tempting, offering the opportunity to return to the ILEA, where I had started my teaching career, and to work with Cathy Avent. I realised that, if I got the job, it would be a life changing moment.

* * *

Originally, interviews were scheduled for the last week in March but had to be postponed for a week, because of rail-strikes and the crisis in the Falklands, where war broke out on 2nd April.

Competition for the two DISCO posts was fierce. When I arrived for the interview, which took place in Divisional Office in Lewisham, and signed in, I read upside down – one of my more useful skills - the names of a long list of candidates. I only recognised one, Dr Jill Key. She taught chemistry in a neighbouring school in Morden and had won a competition to become a Goldsmith's Industrial Fellow. I thought my chances of beating her were minimal.

The interviewing panel consisted of Cathy Avent, and the Inspectors of Secondary Education in Camden and Lewisham. They gave me a stiff grilling. I remember they asked me about my 'industrial experience' which was, of course, nil. Thinking quickly, I referred to my two years' experience as a reporter on the *Church Times*, when I had to produce copy to meet deadlines and had interviewed a range of people in different situations. I also described my work as a careers teacher, my contacts with businesses in the Morden area and my knowledge of economic and industrial history.

Two days later I received a letter from Miss M.F. Adametzi at Division 2, telling me that I was a successful applicant and would be working in Camden and Westminster. I later learned that Jill Key had got the job in Division 7, in Lewisham.

* * *

According to my diary for 1982, I started my new post on Monday, 6th September. On that first day, I took the Northern Line from South Wimbledon all the way up to Warren Street. I crossed the Euston Road, then, leaving the headquarters of Capital Radio on my left, I walked with some trepidation, north along the Hampstead Road, until I reached Netley Street. I don't know what I expected.

What I found was the former house of the caretaker of Netley Primary School. The front door was closed but unlocked. I pushed it open and went inside. I had been told that the two rooms on the ground floor had been assigned to me, one on the right for myself and one on the left for a possible secretary. I peered in. They were both empty, without a desk, a chair or carpet. Even worse, there was no telephone, just two ancient gas fires and bare, dusty floorboards.

I could hear voices upstairs so I went up to see what was happening. On the first floor, I found Hazel King, coordinator of off-site education for disruptive pupils in Division 2. She had a desk, a telephone and a filing cabinet. Her daughter, Oona King,[18] had popped in to see her. She was then a pupil at Haverstock School, along with David and Ed Milliband.

---

[18] Oona King was later elected Labour MP for Tower Hamlets but subsequently defeated by George Galloway, and is now a Labour Peer in the House of Lords.

It was 14 years since I had worked in the ILEA. Then I had been safely installed in Paddington and Maida Vale High School, with numerous supportive colleagues. Now I was on my own in the big wide world. I felt like a goldfish which had been dropped out of its small glass bowl into a fast running stream and might well be swept out to the uncharted waters of the ocean. I returned home at the end of the day, exhausted and bewildered, wondering whether I hadn't been crazy to accept this strange new job rather than the safe post of head of careers and head of history in Morden.

I had an appointment with Cathy Avent on Tuesday, 7th September, at the Careers Education Resource Centre (CERC), at 377 Clapham Road. CERC was on the first floor of an elegant Regency building which also housed the History and Social Sciences' Teachers Centre. I had already been there for a history course, while teaching in Merton. It was to become familiar to me as the base for one of the careers inspectors, Alan Hunwicks, and the careers advisory teachers.

Cathy Avent sympathised with my difficulties about Netley, but told me she had delegated responsibility for the accommodation of the DISCOs, of whom there had been four before Jill Key and I were appointed, to the appropriate divisional officers. She suggested I contact Gwyn Robins, the Divisional Education Officer for Camden and Islington, whose offices were in Oxford Street. I made an appointment on Wednesday, 8th September, with Gwyn Robins and John Hart, his deputy, at 1 pm on the 3rd floor. My diary doesn't record whether I went shopping afterwards but if I did, it was a brief visit only, because I had to get back to Wimbledon for a parent-teachers' meeting at my daughters' comprehensive school, Ricards' Lodge, that evening.

The following week I began to make some key connections. On Monday, I met Ruth Howell from Understanding British Industry (UBI), in Lilley & Skinner's coffee shop in Oxford Street, to discuss how we could work together. Afterwards, I went round the corner to the divisional office to see my new boss, Bill Gowland, the Divisional Inspector for Secondary schools. Two days later, I visited the Camden Careers Office in Kentish Town Road, where I was warmly welcomed by Val Gibson, the Chief Careers Officer and her deputy Carol Smith, both of whom were to be important allies.

My office accommodation had still not been sorted but Barbara Gains, from divisional office, came to Netley, listened to my tale of woe and began to take action on my behalf. Four weeks later, on 29th September 1982 I wrote to Cathy Avent, saying:

> 'My working conditions have improved. My telephone has been connected; my rooms are being painted; someone in DE 14 is working on my funding (I hope) and I think I have found a clerical assistant.'

This was my wonderful secretary, Ann Stockwell, who transformed my life, though she only worked for me part time. My furniture finally arrived in November, though I was still without files or heating.

In the spring of 1983 I wrote: 'The Netley old school-keeper's house has caused problems. There have been fumes from gas fires, causing sickness. There has been no progress on the telephone (switchboard) and the garden is still untended. However, the building has been rewired and I now have a carpet.'

When Hilary Rubenstein, the 16-19 Co-ordinator for Camden and Westminster, joined us in Netley in the summer of 1983, I showed her the room on the top floor and strongly advised her, in the light of my own experience, to write to Bill Gowland, with a list of requirements for her office including a desk, a chair, a filing cabinet, a bookcase and two easy chairs, a gas fire, a budget and a telephone switchboard, with extensions for herself, Hazel King and me, and clerical support. This was provided by Ann Stockwell, who became full time.

Ann's husband, a former garage mechanic, was 'doing the knowledge'- riding about London on a scooter, in preparation for becoming a taxi driver. It was a great day when he drove up outside our office in a black cab.

Ann and her husband were beneficiaries of one Mrs. Thatcher's policies:- the right to buy their council house, at a discount of between 33% and 50% . [19] I was delighted for the Stockwells, personally, but thought it improvident on the part of

---

[19] Andrew Marr; op cit p 430

Central Government to prevent councils from building replacements[20].

*   *   *

ILEA's Division Two was an exciting place in which to work. It covered the City of Westminster and the Borough of Camden. Westminster was the grander of the two, being the site of the Houses of Parliament, Buckingham Palace, the Royal Parks and most of Regent's Park. Westminster Abbey, Westminster Cathedral, the Methodist Central Hall and the temples of commerce in Mayfair and the West End were also within its boundaries.

People from other parts of the metropolis, using London's mainline Victoria station and the underground network, flooded into Westminster each day to work. However, in the north west of the City, there were areas of acute poverty, unemployment and deprivation in health and education, as Humphrey and I saw, when we lived in Notting Hill, in the later 1960s. [21] Within Camden's bounds were Hampstead Heath, the rest of Regent's Park and the Zoo, and Lord's Cricket Ground. Among its buildings were the British Library, and the British Museum. The University of London's headquarters were there and the School of Oriental and African Studies, where Humphrey learnt Chichewa before we went

---

[20] Sadly, I was proved right.

[21] Alan Johnson's biography, *This Boy,* describes growing up there in painful detail. Bantam Press 2013

to Malawi, and two Polytechnics.

Like Westminster, Camden had its centres of poverty: the higher up Hampstead Hill, the better the schools and the housing; the closer to Euston station, the greater the poverty and deprivation. Many of the inhabitants round Netley School were immigrants from Bangladesh and elsewhere, living in bed and breakfast accommodation, but the indigenous white population did not fare much better.

My job was to improve the career prospects for all the young people of the division by providing better links between schools and industry. The question was where to start? In that first year, I identified two priorities: to explore my own division and to learn from the experience of the four people already in the business of setting up school-industry links in other divisions. In November 1982, I wrote a report for the Divisional Inspector, Bill Gowland, which detailed the contacts I had made in Camden and Westminster in the first six weeks since my appointment.

At that stage I had no systematic plan. I was simply looking for people needing assistance and trying to provide it. For example, I helped a sixth form consortium of three schools to find work experience placements for their pupils. I was amazed to discover they were running a course which required the pupils to go on work experience, but none of the teachers had ever found placements or knew how to set about doing so. Each expected the other two to identify the placements but their timetables prevented all of them from visiting firms and asking them to take students on work experience.

I supplied a number of other schools with curriculum materials and joined working parties on 15-19 Occupational Guidance and the London Record of Achievement. This was largely a way of getting known and identifying needs. I visited Westminster, Paddington and Kingsway-Princeton Colleges of Further Education, to discover the extent of their link and bridging courses, run in co-operation with schools, and I talked to staff at Avery Hill College about life and social skills teaching.

At the same time, I was making contact with the other Divisional Industry School Co-ordinators, (DISCOs). Like Jill Key and me, they had been seconded from schools to act as brokers between education and industry. Where they differed from the two of us was in their membership of the Schools Council Industry Project (SCIP).

Prime Minister James Callaghan had made a speech, at Ruskin College, Oxford, on 18th October 1976 about the lack of relationship between industry and education. Though this was often credited with launching schools industry work, Ian Jamieson and Martin Lightfoot pointed out that:

> The Ruskin speech was not the origin of Schools Council Industry Project, which had been under discussion between the Council and the representatives of the Trades Union Congress (TUC) and the Confederation of British Industry

> (CBI) for at least 18 months…
>
> [However,] 'Between the time of the Ruskin speech until the latter part of 1980 there were a series of reports which addressed, from one perspective or another, the problem of the relationship between schools and industry.'[22]

The ILEA asked the Schools Council Industry Project (SCIP) to establish a post for a schools-industry co-ordinator, Hilary Street, in Wandsworth in 1979. She was based in the Divisional Office and worked to the Divisional Inspector and a steering committee, drawn from members of the Wandsworth Community Trust. In September 1980, she took over Lambeth as well. Kevin Crompton, who taught careers and social studies at Ernest Bevin School in Tooting, worked part-time with her in Lambeth and Wandsworth.

By the time I was appointed in 1982, Hilary Street had moved on. After she left, Kevin worked full time as the Lambeth Industry Schools Project Co-ordinator and Jenny Edwards took over the Wandsworth Project. In an article I wrote for *Contact,* the ILEA Journal, in June 1983, I described a visit I made to Lambeth:

> 'I went with Kevin to Elm Court Special School where he helped to develop a mini-co-operative. The pupils in one class formed themselves into a company which ran a tuck shop, at break. They bought sweets, crisps and soft drinks

---

[22]Ian Jamieson & Martin Lightfoot: Schools Council Working Paper 73 Methuen Educational 1982 pp 13-14

at a local cash and carry and sold them at a profit. I was present at a stocktaking check. The pupils counted the stock which remained and calculated what that represented in financial terms. They then subtracted their outgoings to calculate the profit. Finally the results were presented at a "Board Meeting" of all directors.

'They were disappointed to discover that although the turnover was high, the profit was extremely small. There was a vigorous discussion about the reasons for this. They decided that, in an attempt to attract custom, they had charged too little. They were also afraid that some of the stock had been lost when the shop was left unattended one morning.' [23]

I was fascinated to see how these pupils, with special needs, became absorbed in the discussion about why their takings were so small. I saw for myself how the mini-enterprise was helping them to improve their mathematical knowledge and develop entrepreneurial skills which would be useful when they left school.

*　　*　　*

After a report to the Education Committee on 10th July 1981, ILEA agreed to establish two additional posts in the North East of Inner London. Sean Lawlor was appointed co-ordinator for the Tower

---

[23] *Contact* June 1983

Hamlets Industry Schools' Project. He had set up a school support unit in St Richard of Chichester's School, in Camden, before becoming an advisory teacher with the disruptive pupils' programme. While trying to arrange work experience for off-site pupils, he became aware of SCIP and what it had to offer in methodology as well as its given sphere of industry. [24]

When I attended a two day workshop for teachers and local trade unionists organised by Sean, I discovered that adults as well as pupils could benefit from experiential learning techniques. Twelve teachers and 12 trade unionists took part in the workshop. Our time was divided between discussing what the Trade Union Movement could offer schools and looking at specific strategies. We examined various posters, including one on health and safety in the workplace, and tried to decide whether they belonged on a union board or a management one. This generated a lot of discussion and we began to identify the interests shared by both sides - as well as those which clashed. We also realised how extensive was the range of trade union activities.[25]

Tower Hamlets, where Sean worked, was critically affected by the closure of the London Docks. From its early beginnings in the West India Dock in 1802, London's Docklands had become the

---

[24] I always envied the other DISCOs their membership of SCIP and the support they gained from the network. When, later, the number of DISCOs, was made up to 10, one for each ILEA Division, I made sure we negotiated membership of SCIP for all of them.
[25] ILEA *Contact* ibid

most successful in the world. A quarter of the world's trade came through it. Thousands of people were employed in international trade, warehousing and related industries. However, a change in the way goods were transported fundamentally undermined the Docklands' trade. From the 1970s onwards, most international trade was carried in vast shipping containers, in roll-on/ roll-off ferries or by air–freight. The London Docks were too small for the large ships. By 1980, the docks were empty. Half the land was derelict.

The impact on the local community was huge. Over 80,000 jobs were lost in the Docklands area and there was a decline in the local population. Most of the housing in the area was council owned terraced housing and flats. It had been built in the 19th century. When Michael Heseltine, then Secretary of State for Education established the London Docklands Development Corporation (LDDC) under the Local Government Planning and Land Act of 1980, the LDDC was given ownership of the land. It also had outline planning powers which enabled it to establish Canary Wharf. An Enterprise Zone was set up in the Isle of Dogs in 1982 with certain tax breaks. While regeneration was urgently needed, the impact of the Docklands Development on local people, particularly the council tenants was devastating. Their jobs had gone and now their housing was at risk.

Sean was a member of the Joint Dockland Action Group, which included geography teachers in local schools and students of

A level and BTEC [26] Local Studies. They produced *The Wapping Trail,* which was a guided walk through a particular area, during which pupils taking part could make observations and judgements on the use of buildings.

The Action Group also developed a simulation called *The Lime House Blues.* This dealt with a genuine planning application, though the name had been changed, to convert two derelict warehouses into a single luxury dwelling for a film director. The kit included sketch of the proposals, a planning application and letters from groups involved, such as the Council, the LDDC, the Applicant, the Press and an imaginary Residents' Group.

With Julia Fiehn, a political studies advisory teacher,[27] Sean devised *Radio Docklands*, a challenging in-tray exercise, in which students were invited to produce a 10 minute long radio programme called *News and Views at 7.* The pack contained letters from 'listeners' complaining about the lack of jobs for local people, the impact of compulsory purchase and the high prices of the new houses being built. Also included in the pack were news items about local events, of varying significance, such as a visit from Prince Michael of Kent, and a jumble sale, plus advertisements from local companies, which had to be included

---

[26]In 1984 the Business Education Council and the Technical Education Council merged. BTEC offered work related courses. The First Certificate was a Level 2, equivalent to 2 GCSE at A*-C grades.

[27]For more information about Julia Fiehn's work, see below pp 96 &203

because they 'funded' the station. Students, under pressure of time, had to organise themselves into a team, select a major news story and plan interviews, as well as cope with breaking news. It was an effective way of getting the students to think about and become involved in local issues.

* * *

While Sean and Kevin were experienced DISCOS, the rest of us were new. Jenny Edwards, a geography teacher from Norwood School was seconded to the Wandsworth Industry Schools Project in 1982. The project itself had been running successfully since 1977 under Hilary Street and later Kevin Crompton. WISP differed from the other ILEA projects, in having a full-time work experience co-ordinator in Peter Foster. Not surprisingly, the distinguishing characteristic of the project was the large number of work-experience schemes in Wandsworth schools.

> 'Most young people feel positive about work experience,' Jenny told me. 'They gain…social maturity. The organisation and administration of the schemes involve the enthusiastic teachers prepared to do it.'[28]

Jenny found it harder to arrange for teachers to go on work experience. That required changes in people's attitudes and a flexible school organisation. She quoted as an example, three schools which had been planning role plays and simulations like

[28] ILEA *Contact* ibid

Sean's about trades unions in the work place. Unfortunately, because the teachers had at most a 35 minute period once a week, they couldn't use this training method.

More successful was a summer school for sixth formers at Mayfield School, studying science A levels, which Jenny set up with the help of Jill Key:

> 'They will spend two weeks in laboratories, working with the science support team and their own teachers, producing products for part of their placements and undertaking a variety of research tasks which will also increase contacts between teachers and schools and firms.'[29]

Jill had taught chemistry in Sunderland and then Morden. In 1980 she was offered the Goldsmith' Industrial Fellowship.[30] Seconded to British Telecom and the Midland Bank in her first year, in her second, she taught on the PGCE course at the Institute of Education. Because she learnt so much from her own time in industry, her major work in Lewisham was arranging for secondary school teachers to spend two weeks in industry, followed by a period of curriculum development related to their own subject.

> 'A teacher of textiles is going to Marks and Spencers,' Jill said, 'where she will spend a week looking at their policy and decision making processes in the choice of clothes to

---

[29] ILEA *Contact* idem

[30] It was devised jointly by the Worshipful Company of Goldsmiths, Understanding British Industry, the ILEA, and the Institute of Education

> go on sale in their stores. This secondment will encourage mutual understanding and act as a catalyst for change.' [31]

With the science inspectorate, Jill planned a pilot course for science teachers in the autumn term. It was due to last four days, spread over the term and one day was to be spent in industry.

Farquhar McKay, appointed DISCO in Hackney in May 1983, was even newer to the role than Jenny, Jill and I were. Trained as a teacher in New Zealand, he had taught English and Careers at Morpeth School and Sir John Cass Redcoat School in East London. His ambitions were: 'to help promote in Hackney Schools an understanding of the industrial society we live in. I hope to provide a liaison service between schools and the wider community, which will be useful to both groups.'[32]

I was impressed by the talents and creativity of the other DISCOS. Their enthusiasm for school-industry links was infectious. From them, I learnt the three essential characteristics of my job. The first two were about bridging the gap between schools and industry, by seconding teachers into businesses and then, by bringing adults other than teachers (AOTs) into school. The third characteristic was the encouragement of active learning methods.

The six of us agreed to meet regularly and exchange ideas

---

[31] ILEA *Contact* June 1983 ibid
[32] For examples of Farquhar's innovative work see below pp 95-7 &124-5

and information. The venue was my office in Netley Street, because it was central, and it now even had chairs on which to sit. From time to time, we collaborated on a course. Kevin got funding from the TUC to organise a day's course at the Polytechnic of the South Bank, with a trade unionist. He asked each DISCO to bring a teacher and a trade unionist from our own Division. I was detailed to advertise it in *Contact*. Cathy Avent was enthusiastic and suggested the names of various people to take part. Kevin ran the poster exercise in the morning and we took part in a role play in the afternoon

CHAPTER FIVE

Raising the Profile of School-Industry Links 1982-4

I was beginning to speak at conferences and to run courses – neither of which I had done before. On October 6th 1982, just a month after I had started in my post, I was on the agenda for the Secondary Heads' Conference in Division 2, alongside my new friend, Ruth Howell of UBI. We had been asked to explain our roles and to discuss the help we could offer to schools. That was an easy, low key beginning for something which became increasingly important in my role and the role of all the DISCOs as we spread the gospel of school-industry links.

On 2nd February 1983 I was involved, together with a representative from the Business Education Council, in an evening course, on 16-19 Curriculum Development, at Camden & Westminster Teachers' Centre. Because it was outside school hours, I was paid a fee of £21.88. It seems a small amount now, but it felt large then.

By 22nd November1983, I was speaking at a conference on 'The Gateway to Employment', hosted by Councillor William C. Smith JP, Chairman of the Association for Careers and Employment in Inner West London. The other speakers were

Cathy Avent and Ruth Howell. The audience was made up of teachers, lecturers, from the schools and colleges, careers officers, and employers. I was asked to take part because Division 1, Kensington & Chelsea, still had no DISCO and was lobbying for one.

In the early stages, I wrote out my speeches in full - I still have the handwritten text of one. As I grew more confident, I spoke extempore, using cards with prompts. I used my speeches to question the stereotypes which schools had about industry – that it was a dirty, noisy, boring place in which human values were subordinated to the profit motive and bosses grew fat on expense account lunches in their wall-to-wall carpeted offices, while their employees contracted industrial diseases such as asbestosis.

I concluded that one of the most serious consequences of these stereotypes was that for close on 200 years middle class English boys had been sent to public schools, where they were not taught science or engineering, though their fathers might have made their money as engineers and industrialists. Instead they studied Latin and Greek,[33] which prepared them for administration in the UK and the Colonies. As a result, other countries, like Germany overtook us in technical developments.

I spoke about boys' education because I was talking to

---

[33] When Macaulay introduced entry to the Civil Service by examination in 1845, applicants discovered that the best preparation for the exam. was to have studied Greats at Oxford.

audiences of business men, but in the 19th century, most women only had access to elementary education, in board schools, after 1870. The daughters of the wealthy were taught by governesses or went to schools founded by pioneers, like Miss Beale and Miss Buss, which followed a curriculum not dissimilar to that in boys' public schools.

I also sought to challenge employers' stereotypes of education - that teachers were a lot of long-haired Marxists layabouts, who only worked 40 weeks a year; were hostile to the wealth producing section of society and dismally failed to inculcate the three Rs into their pupils.

By arranging for teachers and students to go into industry and for business people to become involved with schools, I hoped to bring the two sides together. Breaking down the stereotypes would, I believed, improve the life chances of the young people in schools and colleges. It wasn't easy, however, to organise these exchanges in a time of recession. My article for the ILEA newspaper *Contact*, began with an account of the economic situation:

> 'Youth unemployment in Division 2 [Camden & Westminster] doubled in two years and long term youth unemployment of six months or more [went] up by a factor of 7… The Manpower Services Commission (MSC) was circulating its proposals for the Youth Training Scheme (YTS) and the new Technical and Vocational Education

> Initiative (TVEI) for 14-18 year olds was suddenly announced.[34] At the same time many small businesses were going bankrupt and even multi-nationals were moving their headquarters out of the centre of London. There were occasions, therefore when I wondered whether the whole field of industry-schools liaison was not a quicksand which would swallow any edifice constructed on its quaking surface.'[35]

Though unemployment and poverty was high in some areas, both in a geographical and occupational sense, I didn't have to cope in Camden and Westminster, with the industrial desert which my DISCO colleagues faced elsewhere. Division 2 contained a variety of workplaces, from the head offices of trade unions, including Arthur Scargill's miners, to the headquarters of multi-national companies; from the huge railway terminals of Euston and Kings Cross, to radio and television studios; from major teaching hospitals, like the Royal Free and University College Hospital, to small clothing factories.

There were also a number of colleges of further and higher education, in the Division, including the Polytechnic of Central London in Marylebone Road. Professor John Stansgate and I

---

[34] TVEI was reputedly the brainchild of Sir Keith Joseph who had seen something similar in France. At the beginning, it was lavishly funded by David Young at the MSC, bypassing both the Department of Employment (DOE) and the cash strapped Department for Education and Science (DES).
[35] ILEA *Contact* June 1983

discovered that we had both grown up in Handsworth, in Birmingham. John had failed his 11 plus, while I had been coached and passed mine, going to King Edward VI's High School. Despite that, it was he who was now an academic. He ran a course for Division 2 teachers wanting to set up mini-enterprises in schools. This was funded by the Department for Trade and Industry, which was also involved in getting computers into schools.

The vigorous, forward-looking leadership of Val Benson, the Divisional Careers Officer, and her deputy and successor, Carol Smith, was a tremendous bonus for me. On my first visit to the careers office, I saw a sign on one door which read 'Liz Shields.' I was intrigued because that was the married name of one of my close friends at St Hilda's, Oxford. I took a chance and put my head round the door.

I was delighted to discover it was my friend, Liz, who was working there as Quadrant Employment Liaison Officer. She and I collaborated with John Hart, the Deputy Divisional Education Officer, on the production of a resource guide for teachers and careers officers. I owed many of my early contacts with industrialists to Carol and Liz. In return, when I organised meetings for teachers and employers, I invited careers officers to join us.

The Careers and Training Association brought together careers officers, teachers and lecturers from F.E. colleges. Its steering committee consisted of Michael Joyce, careers teacher at Hampstead School, [36] Janet Lunzer, a careers officer, and me. Our termly meetings dealt with the new Youth Training Scheme (YTS), unemployment, new technology and women's employment. In Camden's Information Technology Education Centre (ITEC), I met the Assistant Manager, Priscilla Waller, who had been at the Oxford High School with me.[37] Together we planned a workshop for schools about the impact of information technology on employment. The purpose was to make pupils aware of the economic community in which they lived.

Many companies offered generous facilities. For instance, the London Electricity Board (LEB) ran a series of workshops for 14 year olds on the use of electricity at home and in business. They used active learning methods, involved adults other than teachers and took place on the LEB's own premises.

A different approach was used by the Grubb Institute for their innovative *Transition to Working Life* (TWL) scheme, which had been developed, with Manpower Services Commission funding. It was already operating in Islington and in four Camden schools when I arrived. 'Coaches' were recruited from industry, for example, British Gas, to work with small groups of vulnerable

---

[36] Michael Joyce was my eventual successor as DISCO for Camden & Westminster

[37] I transferred there, aged 14, when my family moved from Birmingham to Oxford.

young people in schools. They met, off the school premises, with their coach for half a day a week for 16 weeks and designed their own programme of visits to workplaces and discussions about the problems which arose at work. I was delighted when John Bazalgette, from the Grubb Institute, invited me to attend the steering groups at Haverstock and Pimlico Schools.

TWL was used with sixth formers but it was particularly successful with 5th year pupils, alienated from school. As a result of taking part in TWL, their behaviour towards adults and other pupils changed markedly. Each project school appointed a teacher to be their TWL adviser, to liaise with the working coach and to be secretary of the steering group which included teachers, governors and representatives of the local economy. Carol Woolley, the TWL co-ordinator, worked from my office, to support the Project. Tony Wingate, an advisory head, had overall responsibility for the project.

The funding for Carol's post wasn't always secure and for a short period in 1983 it stopped altogether, so I had to do her work as well as my own. Despite this, the project was expanding and a number of new schools were anxious to join. David Chambers, a new member of Cathy Avent's team of Careers Inspectors, held an induction workshop for new TWL teachers in November 1983 at the Camden Teachers' Centre.

Hazel King, my Netley neighbour, identified off-site units, for pupils excluded from mainstream schools, which were keen to develop mini-enterprises. She put me in touch with Nick Peacey, who was in charge of the Bourne, in Margaret Street. Nick taught his students how to run a committee meeting effectively – a skill he said would stand them in good stead in their adult lives. He recruited a bank manager to help them keep accounts.

I watched, amazed, as these former disruptive pupils, learnt to 'address the chair' and to take turns in putting forward their ideas, instead of all shouting at once. They made a video about the dangers of nuclear weapons[38] and advertised it to local schools, which they charged to view it. They gave carefully prepared speeches, introducing the film, a remarkable achievement for teenage lads, who had been accustomed to communicate only in grunts.

Another off-site unit which I visited was called the Spark Project. It was run by a woman, whose name I have sadly forgotten. She invited me to lunch. She had in her care a bunch of strapping lads from the East End of London, dressed in the height of fashion. Their jeans, sweat shirts and watches must have fallen off the back of a lorry - or else were extremely clever copies. We sat round the table, over which she presided like a Nanny in a large country house. She reminded the lads of their manners, making sure they held their knives and forks properly, passed dishes round

---

[38] This was a very hot topic at the time as waste from nuclear power stations passed through London by train at night.

and encouraged them to make conversation with me. Afterwards, she said to me most of them had never sat down at a table to eat a communal meal before coming to the Project.

*   *   *

At the end of my first year in post, my report to Cathy Avent and the DI, Bill Gowland, focused on the matching of teachers with representatives of the economic community. I described the meetings I had arranged between staff from Camden libraries, school librarians, careers teachers and officers, in an effort to improve the range and quality of careers information in schools. Mrs. Mulligan, the advisory teacher for textiles, and I brought together home economics teachers and the staff of Marks and Spencers in Kilburn as a first stage in developing contacts and secondments. Members of the school of management at the Polytechnic of Central London had a session with heads and deputies to discuss teaching entrepreneurial skills to pupils.

Two workshops for the Careers and Training Association, which I organised, involved both teachers and careers officers. One prepared pupils for the possibility of unemployment; the other focused on the uses of micro-technology. With the further education work-experience co-ordinator, I visited the majority of schools and talked to teachers in charge of work experience. Together, we arranged the first meeting for representatives from all the schools to discuss how to set up placements, at a time of high unemployment, and how to share and maintain them.

I also negotiated teacher secondments to industry, putting Mr. Craven, the head of mathematics at Haverstock, in touch with Sainsbury's about their management skills course, and organised a four week secondment with BP, for Mr. Gilligan, of Sir William Collins.

My 1983 report showed how far schools-industry links had progressed in Camden, in the past year. I was now concentrating on creating direct links between subject teachers and the local economic community which would lead to curriculum development and the use of a variety of teaching strategies. I felt like a marriage broker, as I matched community resources to the needs of individual schools, arranging meetings between teachers and industrialists, who discussed courses for pupils, the production of materials, and secondments to industry.

School–industry links were also beginning to have a much higher profile, right across the ILEA. In March 1983, I received a letter from Barbara Gains,[39] who had been appointed secretary to the newly established Committee on the Curriculum and Organisation of Secondary Schools, (CCOSS), chaired by Dr David Hargreaves, then Reader in Education at the University of Oxford. He had been invited to take on the role by ILEA's radical leader, Frances Morrell, who wanted to raise standards in ILEA schools.

---

[39] Barbara had sorted out my furniture and I was eternally grateful to her.

CCOSS took evidence from a wide range of people, including the DISCOs. Barbara asked me to submit, by the end of term, a paper about the impact of schools-industry work on education. The timing was tight but I daren't miss the opportunity. I put everything else on hold and wrote furiously, which resulted in a two page summary, backed up by a four page report. I began by pointing out that I had only been in post for six months and so was still in the process of exploring Division 2. Despite this, I identified two factors for change.

First, the amalgamation of grammar and secondary schools to form comprehensives had forced teachers to reassess their provision for pupils of lower ability. Second, the advent of the YTS [40]was perceived as a threat which might affect sixth forms. I suggested that some radical methods of organisational development used in industry, such as learning circles, in which managers and shop floor workers met as equals and discussed changes in practice, could be adopted by schools to cope with these changes.

I then outlined ways of re-motivating under-achieving children. As work experience placements became increasingly scarce, schools were looking at alternatives, such as teacher

---

[40] YTS : The Youth Training Scheme, an on-the-job training scheme for school leavers aged 16-17, managed by the Manpower Services Commission, started in 1983. Initially, it was for one year only but in 1986 was extended to two years.

secondment; industry organised courses and visits, work shadowing and work simulations, including mini-companies. I described, in detail, the Grubb Institute's TWL scheme, which used people from industry to "coach" school students about the world of work. I concluded by saying that the common elements of all these initiatives were the development in young people of personal skills, basic literacy and numeracy as well as an understanding of industry.

Barbara Gains wrote, thanking me for my helpful evidence and asking me and my DISCO Colleagues to meet a group of members of CCOSS at County Hall on 22 September to continue the discussion. Of course we jumped at the opportunity.

Dr Hargreaves's report, *Improving Secondary Schools,* published in 1984, was based on all the evidence submitted to his committee. It became the ILEA New Testament. To our delight, it contained an entire section on 'Schools, Industry and the Trades Unions.'

This had obviously been written after a vigorous discussion in the Committee. Some members were clearly afraid that schools–industry work might lead to a narrowing and even a potential dumbing down of the curriculum. They darkly suspected the motives of industrialists who became involved with schools. As a result, the Committee felt it necessary to re-iterate its own:

> 'opposition to a strong vocational bias before the age of 16 because this constrains future choice and threatens the

> principle of a broad curriculum for all pupils during the period of compulsory education. However, we believe that all pupils should, before the age of 16 be provided with opportunities to acquire knowledge and skills relevant to adult life and employment.'[41]

The Committee warned, in paragraph 3.15.3 that, despite the change of attitude towards school-industry initiatives, this did not always lead to changes in the formal curriculum:

> 'Too often links with industry are seen as relevant only to low achieving pupils. Too often they are confined to the crevices and corners of the curriculum, though visits to workplaces may well enlarge the experience of both teachers and pupils and thus make classroom lessons more interesting and relevant.'

The relevance of school-industry links to the curriculum and their effect on pupils was noted in paragraph 3.15.4:

> 'Some teachers told us that they sought closer links with the world of work because it motivated pupils in a way which "normal school" did not, and that it often produced a renewal of parental interest. The motives of another group of teachers were to gain access to resources, information, opinions and experience not usually available within the school to enliven and update subject teaching. For some

---

[41] *Improving Secondary Schools*: ILEA March 1984 p85 para 3.15.2

> subjects, eg science, commerce and, particularly, careers there are immediate benefits to be gained.'

In the same paragraph, the Committee declared that:

> 'Sharp questions must continually be asked about the motives and objectives of (employers and trades unionists) forging the links, but we are convinced that the overall effect of such liaison has been to open up ILEA schools to the surrounding community in ways which may benefit teachers as much as pupils.
>
> 'The sharp decline in the fortunes of British industry generated in some industrialists considerable hostility towards the comprehensive school curriculum, blame being apportioned simultaneously *both* for an assumed decline in academic standards and an over-concentration on academic as opposed to practical and vocational skills. We are told, however, that attitudes change as dialogue continues between industrialists, trades unions and teachers.'[42]

The 81st of the 104 recommendations made by CCOSS was that the Chief Inspector should:

> 'establish a committee of the 10 divisional industry school co-ordinators and the staff inspectors for science; craft design and technology; careers; geography and social science to review present practice and to disseminate good

---

[42] Idem para 3.15.6

practice.'[43]

I have no minutes of this committee's meetings in my files, but the DISCO numbers were made up to 10 and they certainly collaborated with the all staff inspectors mentioned in the Hargreaves Report.

* * *

In July 1983, I attended Division 2's annual conference, held at Garnett College, Roehampton. On the Friday night, Frances Morrell was the main speaker. She had been an assistant to Tony Benn. In 1979, she stood successfully for the Greater London Council. As an Inner London member she automatically became a member of the Inner London Education Authority (ILEA) and in 1983 she was elected leader. There were many people who criticised her for being too radical and for failing to tackle the surplus of teachers in schools with falling rolls but she was a most inspiring speaker. Her theme at the divisional conference was 'ILEA Policies and Priorities.'

One of Frances Morell's key priorities was to raise standards of teaching and learning in ILEA schools. It was she who head hunted Dr Hargreaves to become Chief Inspector to carry out that policy.

'The inspectorate was seen by ILEA Members as the key

[43] Idem p119

instrument in the field of school improvement.'[44]

I was told that the Greater London Council (GLC) paid for the ILEA schools out of the rates it levied on Londoners and received no subsidy from the Government. As a result, it was able to carry out its own policies, which were regarded as spendthrift and socialist by the Conservatives. However, as long as the GLC existed, the ILEA felt safe.

*   *   *

By the beginning of September 1983, I was conscious that the pattern of my work had altered. I no longer had to search out new opportunities. Instead, practitioners were approaching me, inviting me to help with their own curriculum change. For example, I was asked to collaborate with the Further and Higher Curriculum Development Unit at Westminster College and with work-experience co-ordinators from the further education colleges at Paddington, Kingsway-Princeton and North London. Together we ran a workshop for teachers and lecturers on designing their own curriculum materials. With some of my DISCO colleagues, I met the Staff Inspector for Design and Technology (D&T) and the Warden of the D & T Teachers' centre to plan an entrepreneurs' summer school.

---

[44] A. Radford ' An Enquiry into the Abolition of the Inner London Education Authority (1964 to 1988), with Particular Reference To Politics and Policy Making'. A thesis submitted for the degree of PhD, University of Bath ,Department of Education, June 2009

I linked home economics and textiles teachers with Marks & Spencer's, where I learnt some useful tips about washing clothes, and the London Fashion Centre, which was hosting a fascinating exhibition of young designers' work. Places on management courses were offered to teachers by British Rail, with whom I had an excellent contact in Danny Giblin, who showed me round the moth-balled St Pancras Hotel.

There were other signs that the schools-industry movement was beginning to attract wider attention. When Dr John Stansgate from the Polytechnic of Central London and I agreed to organise a course for teachers on mini-enterprises, representatives from the Department of Trade and Industry (DTI) and the London Enterprise Agency (LEntA) turned up at our second meeting. I had no idea, at the time, how significant these two organisations would become in the development of schools-industry links across the ILEA.

However, while the seedlings of curriculum innovation flourished in the fertile ground of Camden, I found it much more difficult to make progress in Westminster. Camden Borough Council and the City of Westminster had radically different economic and political attitudes. The officials of both boroughs were personally anxious to establish good liaison with schools. In Westminster, for example, officials of the town planning department and the libraries were helpful and interested in developing schools industry links, even if the elected members were not.

I did, however, succeed in establishing good contacts with Esso in Victoria, which ran a computing studies course for pupils and teachers in three Westminster Schools, which I attended. The two boys' schools were deeply committed to the project. Sadly, this was less true of the one girls' school.

In the early 1980s, main frame computers were giant machines, the size of a small family car. They filled whole rooms, were kept at low temperatures, and data was stored on tape kept in tins the size of car wheels. It was exciting to hear Esso staff talking about the development of desk top computers for the most senior staff members in the near future. It seemed impossible that one day I would have a computer on my desk.

I also made contact with Professor Robert Kowalski of Imperial College[45]. He talked about the future possibilities of shopping on the Internet or researching one's ancestry, which seemed mind blowing at the time.

Unfortunately, I wasn't able to follow that lead up because, when I had a conversation with Cathy Avent about the possibility of collaborating with him, I was told the ILEA was already committed to working with JIIG-CAL, (Job Ideas and Information Generator- Computer Assisted Learning). This was an early batch

---

[45] His daughter, Danya, and my daughter, Katy, were in the same class at Ricards' Lodge, a comprehensive school in Wimbledon.

– processing computerised careers programme, matching pupils' talents, interests and capabilities with the requirement of jobs. Pupils keyed in their interests and the examinations they were studying for and got back a print-out which gave them details of jobs they might like to apply for. It was useful in focussing pupils' minds but sometimes the results were surprising. When I tried the programme out myself it suggested I might like to be an advertising agent, which was one of the things I would least like to have done.

Despite my best efforts, I was never able to engage with the City of Westminster in the same way as I did with Camden, which had an active economic development unit, headed by Christine Wray. Its officers staffed the youth employment committee and the voluntary youth employment group, chaired by Kate Hoey.[46] When she left, the chair was taken by Gwyn Robins, the Divisional Officer, himself. It was a useful forum for discussing the problems of youth unemployment, as its membership included Carol Harrison, from the Careers Service.

Camden's Town Planning Department published economic and social notes about the composition of Camden which were a valuable source of information. Two of its members, John Newby and Felicity Robinson, had particular responsibility for liaison with

---

[46] Kate Hoey resigned to 'nurse' her prospective constituency in Vauxhall. She was elected as the Labour MP there, on 15 June 1989.

schools. They became involved in planning, resourcing and running a development game for the liberal studies programme in the sixth form of Sir William Collins' School.

As a result of talks with Divisional Office, it was agreed to produce an economic and social profile of the borough which could be used both in the classroom and in the careers office as a way of alerting young people to the economic situation outside the school gates. Tony Grundy, a peripatetic teacher in Division 2, was seconded to edit the information and create the Camden Pack and to work towards producing a similar profile of Westminster.

The Camden Pack was an item on the agenda of the last meeting of the youth employment group which I attended on 9 March 1984. That same month I wrote my final report on schools industry links in Division 2, emphasising how lucky I had been in having the support and co-operation of the town planning department and also of the Careers Office, in everything I did. The Careers and Training Association had termly meetings dealing with such issues as YTS, unemployment, new technology and women's employment.

I had also gained a great deal of help from voluntary agencies such as the Camden Council and Westminster Voluntary Action for Social Services and the Youth Agencies. I acknowledged that some of my initiatives had been less successful than others. Some events, which happened almost by chance, proved to be extremely productive. For example, the arrival of the

16-19 co-ordinator, Hilary Rosenthal, my Netley neighbour, marked the beginning of a useful co-operation.

I concluded: 'The 20 months I have spent in Division 2 have been extremely stimulating and exciting. In part, this has been the natural result of any new job; in part the quite astonishing welcome I received in schools and industry; but mostly the nature of the job itself which has been pioneering and innovative.'

CHAPTER SIX

Inspector for Careers Education & Schools Industry Links 1984-1987

In 1984, Alan Hunwicks, one of Cathy Avent's team of Careers Inspectors, resigned in 1984, to go to Surrey as an Assistant Education Officer. After much heart searching, I decided to apply for his job,

I loved the hands-on nature of the DISCO job in Division 2 and the freedom which I had enjoyed to plan my own work. At the end of two years, I was beginning to see the fruits of experiential learning and the closer links between schools and industry. I knew infinitely more about education, commerce and industry than when I started. I had learnt a great deal from my DISCO colleagues and had developed new skills. Did I really want to give up this amazing DISCO job? No, but I thought that as a careers inspector, I could continue to support these developments and might also have a wider remit.

On 25 January 1984, I was interviewed for the post of careers inspector in the ILEA. Cathy told me later that I had interviewed 'conspicuously well', but when she came to sum up the candidates she was surprised to have her attention drawn to one section on my application form, which asked why I had left my previous jobs. Usually people wrote ‘promotion’ or ‘maternity leave’. I had explained my reason for leaving my teaching post in Malawi with the laconic statement ‘husband deported.’

Humphrey, who was then Rector of the Anglican Church in Lilongwe, was deported because he had visited and ministered to political prisoners, who were held, without trial in one of the detention centres in his parish[47]. However, the answer created some doubts about my suitability.

Cathy Avent’s boss, Trevor Jaggar , Senior Staff Inspector for Secondary Schools, who had spent time in Tanzania as a district officer, asked: ‘Is this all right?’

Cathy, who knew nothing of the government in Malawi, said: ‘Oh yes, right-wing regime.’ She was correct in her guess. Dr Banda, originally the liberator of his country from colonial rule, had become a dictator.

I received a letter from D.G. Taylor Head of Personnel Services Division saying: ‘Following your interview… I am pleased to confirm the decision of the interviewing panel to offer you the post of inspector for careers education in the grade of Senior Officer Band 6 … You will be based initially at County Hall. Your commencing salary will be basic annual salary of

---

[47] On his return to the UK he reported on conditions in the detention centres to Amnesty International.

£13,812 (under review) plus £1,284 London Weighting Allowance… following an assessment, incremental progression is payable on 1 April each year.'

Delighted though I was to have been appointed, saying goodbye to my friends and colleagues in Camden and Westminster and the other members of the Netley Staff was painful. I deeply regretted leaving my secretary, Ann Stockwell, and Carol Woolley, the TWL Co-ordinator, but I am sure they were well looked after by my successor as DISCO for Division 2, Michael Joyce. Originally a physics teacher, I knew him as head of careers at Hampstead School and part of the Careers Association Committee.

* * *

Cathy Avent's letter of 26th January 1984, announcing my appointment to all the DISCOS, said: 'I know you will all be delighted to know that Anne Taylor was successful at the interviews for Alan Hunwicks' job as inspector for careers education and guidance. We do not expect her to transfer until 1st May but we hope to get the advertisement for her replacement out as fast as possible so that can be filled as well as Kevin's vacancy in Division 9.' [48] Cathy also wrote to welcome me to her little team, saying how much she and David Chambers looked forward to my arrival.

---

[48] Kevin Crompton went to the University of Warwick, which had the Schools Council Industry Project archive.

David was a gentle giant, well over six feet tall. He was a product of the ILEA, having been at Haberdashers' Aske School. He had done non-graduate teacher training but took a degree at King's College, London, while working, and was given a year's study leave by the ILEA to complete his degree. He lived in Hertfordshire with his wife, who was P.A. to a Head of Department at Hatfield Polytechnic, and their sons. He once confessed to me, that he had a passion for buying first editions, especially Henry James' novels.

Originally, David had taught art at Booke House, a 1000 strong boys' school in Hackney. Denis Felsenstein, who was head there before joining the inspectorate, first as a divisional inspector, and later as Senior Staff Inspector for Secondary Schools, told me that the art department: 'was probably the best department in the school not only for the quality of its work, but for its support and compassion for young people in Hackney, with a multitude of problems. David stood out as one of the most caring teachers in the school.'[49]

Undoubtedly for this reason, David was put in charge of careers there. He was so successful that Cathy Avent appointed him as a careers advisory teacher from 1981-1982, to work with her and her colleague, Alan Hunwicks. In 1983, because of the great expansion of careers work, Cathy was able to secure a third

[49] Denis Felsenstein, letter to Anne Dart Taylor 07.07. 2014

inspectorate post, to which David was appointed.

With my arrival, David, who had been based in County Hall, moved to the Careers Education and Resources Centre (CERC) at 377, Clapham Road. I took over his desk in the room[50] next to Cathy's for the first two terms, after my appointment, so Cathy, as she put it in a letter to me, could give me 'such training as our rather disjointed lives can provide.'

I had organised my own induction to the DISCO job in Camden, by talking to more experienced DISCOS and by arranging meetings with key people in Camden and Westminster. The programme for new inspectors was more formal, as was to be expected in the second largest education authority in the UK. [51] I was privileged to attend a course run by Tony Travers, [52] an academic and journalist specialising in issues affecting local government. He gave us mind-blowing figures about the ILEA budget and also, by using role play, taught us ways of negotiating with trade unions. I remember demonstrating to everyone how *not* to do it by becoming confrontational and raising the stakes. It was a useful lesson to me, as well as to others present, about defusing conflict.

In her letter of 30th January 1984, Cathy Avent wrote: 'You

---

[50] I shared the room with two further education inspectors.
[51] The largest was Strathclyde.
[52] Professor Tony Travers is director of LSE London, a research centre at the London School of Economics. He is also a visiting professor in the LSE's Government Department.

will receive various documents from Trevor Jaggar and you will also be told about the induction scheme for new inspectors. You need to know about governors' meetings, disciplinary questions, quinquennial reviews and so forth…During the summer term, therefore, you will take part in a series of induction visits to different branches here so as to understand more about the way the inspectorate and administration work and I will arrange for you to make some special visits for example to the Learning Materials Service, the Publishing and TV centres, CUES,[53] [and] the headquarters of the careers service and I shall take you to governors' meetings so that you get the hang of the inspector's role at them.

'We are applying for a place for you on the JIIG-CAL trainers' course at Edinburgh which runs from 26th-30 March and that will give you the immediate opportunity to help with the summer JIIG-Cal course…'

I wasn't pleased that the course dates meant I should be away from home on my birthday. However I dutifully went to Edinburgh, a city which I had only visited previously in August, during the Festival and the Fringe, when it was crammed with sightseers, actors, artists, comedians, musicians, and playwrights. On those occasions, I had stayed in East Lothian with my friends,

[53] The Centre for Urban Educational Studies; ILEA'S centre for education in a multi-ethnic society,

Sari and Robin Salvesen, who had both been at Oxford with me, and played tennis at 11 pm, in the long, light evenings of a Scottish summer.

In March, Edinburgh was a dour and chilly city, its elegant granite buildings only occasionally illuminated by the fitful spring sunshine. I was staying in basic student accommodation at the University and had little opportunity to explore, as the course took up most of my time. I duly completed my training and returned to London prepared to hand on my newly acquired knowledge to careers teachers and to begin my duties as a careers inspector.

'We work out at the beginning of each term,' Cathy Avent told me, 'a programme of activities for ourselves and we try to ensure, particularly in the spring, when 'flu sometimes upsets programmes, that we do not have commitments of equal importance on the same day so that if one or other of us is ill, someone else can substitute. Otherwise, you work out your own programme. Priorities go to meetings of governors, full inspections of schools and colleges (normally only one a term but taking up much of two to three weeks), quinquennial reviews, courses for teachers and then the normal pastoral visits to encourage careers teachers or to cajole heads into providing better facilities.'

Cathy was anxious that I should be aware that: 'we have one or two particular delicacies because of our previous connection with the Careers Service.' She had been the Principal Careers Officer for the ILEA before becoming the first Careers Inspector for schools. Therefore she ruled that 'we do not ourselves inspect careers officers and are not in any way concerned to press their claims for time or facilities in schools…We do not use them as spies for information about what is happening in the schools and normally only talk to them after we have completed a full inspection and not before, so that what we see the teachers doing is unbiased by any criticism the careers officer may wish to voice… If I get some criticism of (careers officers) I refer the matter to Pat White.'[54]

Like many teams of inspectors, we divided London geographically. David Chambers, who lived in St Albans, took prior responsibility for the eastern divisions of the ILEA, namely Islington, Hackney, Tower Hamlets, Greenwich and Lewisham. By a fortunate chance, my predecessor, Alan Hunwicks, had lived in Surrey, as I did, and looked after the western divisions, Kensington & Chelsea, Camden & Westminster, Wandsworth, Lambeth and Southwark, which Cathy now allocated to me.

This was only in connection with what Cathy called 'pastoral visiting', that is a visit to the school to look at the provision of careers education and to report to the head. As she explained: 'We all take part in full inspections and must be free to attend governors' meetings wherever they occur. I normally do the bulk of the evening governors' meetings because I do not have a

---

[54] Mrs. Pat White was the Principal Careers Officer for the ILEA.

family awaiting my attentions. The advisory teacher can do normal visits to newly appointed careers teachers or those having difficulties over materials or programmes. An advisory teacher does not attend governors' meetings or normally try to persuade heads of the need for better resources or timetabling (as inspectors do).'

Cathy was also keen to emphasise that: 'At governors' meetings or full inspections it is important that we function in exactly the same way as other subject inspectors. We do not make value judgements on a teacher's performance without adequate opportunity to observe it nor do we ourselves recommend appointments at a governors' meeting. Our function is to ask candidates the technical questions about the teaching of the subject, to clarify points of doubt on the application form and to sum up as fairly as possible, indicating if there are candidates who do not appear to have adequate qualifications or experience for the job, but avoiding any appearance of having ourselves decided who should get it. I use these occasions to enlighten governors on the real purpose of careers education since many of them do not understand the difference between the job of a careers teacher and that of a careers officer and I try to look as though I am enjoying it and to make the governors feel that they are enjoying the evening too.'

I am sure she succeeded because Cathy was a lively and entertaining speaker, with a fund of amusing stories.

* * *

After I had passed my medical, I moved into County Hall. In 1984, which was an exciting place in which to work. It was like a small town, with its medical services, its cafes and restaurants, its council chambers, its meeting rooms and the hundreds of offices where its 8,000 inhabitants worked. It was then the headquarters of the Greater London Council (GLC), it ran the fire service, emergency planning, waste disposal and flood prevention throughout the capital and shared responsibility for providing roads, housing, city planning and leisure services with the boroughs. In addition, from 1970 to 1984 it had control of public transport.

'Red' Ken Livingstone, the leader of the GLC was hugely active, provoking liking and loathing in equal measure. His socialist policies brought him into direct conflict with the conservative government of Margaret Thatcher. For example, he used government subsidies to reduce tube and bus fares. He met Gerry Adams, the Sinn Fein leader, who was banned from entering Britain, and supported the creation of a statue of Nelson Mandela, which was often vandalised. He ran anti-racist courses for young people, one of which was attended by my elder daughter, Katy. He regularly posted banners of the latest unemployment figures for London on the side of County Hall. They were clearly visible across the Thames, from the Houses of Parliament and were a constant irritant to Mrs. Thatcher.

County Hall was where Cathy Avent had her office and where I was based for two terms. On my first visit, Cathy spent an hour talking me through the role of an inspector and the protocols of visiting schools. We must not arrive unannounced. Instead, we should request a visit in advance, give feedback at the time and send a written report to the head, afterwards. She showed me copies of the letters she had sent. Cathy had been a careers officer and not a teacher so she did not observe lessons on her visits. Instead, she discussed with the heads matters relating to departmental capitation and resources of money and time.

Cathy took me along to meet the new Chief Inspector, Dr Hargreaves. He gave me my brown briefcase, which all ILEA inspectors carried, and wished me well. I was photographed for my name badge and collected my pass, which gave me entry to the car park in front of County Hall, and I was introduced to Nina Towndrow, the doyenne of the secretaries and the typing pool, in room 281.

I was now an ILEA inspector. I was even more nervous than I had been when starting the DISCO job. In retrospect, I realised, Division 2 had been a manageable area. The field in which I was about to operate was much larger. I knew the schools in Camden and Westminster but had never set foot in those in the other four divisions for which I had just become responsible. I needed to find my way around them. We did not have sat-nav.s in those days, just the London A-Z.

Sometimes, it was more convenient to travel by underground than by car and I became expert at judging how long such a journey would take. In the days, when Ken Livingstone ran transport, there seemed to be fewer breakdowns.

In 1984 and 1985, as I exited the tube stations I frequently saw miners with collecting buckets. They were on strike against the Coal Board's proposed pit closures. I always gave them money. My brother John's wife, Christine Newman, was the daughter of a Yorkshire miner, so I knew how hard they were hit. Newspapers and television covered horrifying scenes of battles between miners and police.

More often, I travelled across London by car. Occasionally, I wrote in my diary the details of a long day of '9 hrs 30 mins' or a long drive- '36 miles'- in my white Fiat 600 . At least it was bigger and more comfortable than the Fiat 500 and less likely to be run down by lorries. Also, I didn't have to double de-clutch to change gears.

We had to fill in forms, listing our hours of work and our mileage, for which we could claim petrol money. Those forms may be languishing somewhere in the basement of the Institute of Education,[55] or they may have been put on a bonfire. However, I have a couple of photocopies lurking in my files. They date from 1989 and cover four weeks. On average, I worked 62 hours per

---

[55] ILEA files were deposited in the Institute after the Abolition.

week - though this fluctuated between '84 hrs 30 mins', in a week when I was running two in-service training courses, and a mere 38 hours, when I spent two days in Dunraven School, in Lambeth, on an inspection. Of course, I then had to spend several hours writing up my findings at home.

I drove 528 miles in those four weeks. Again, there were wide variations. One week my mileage was just 68, as I only went to the Careers Education Resources Centre (CERC) in Clapham, County Hall, near Waterloo, and Dunraven School in Lambeth. The following week the total was 380 miles because I visited Hampstead School, in Camden, and Elizabeth Garrett Anderson School, in Islington; attended a Compact Conference in County Hall; and went to the Institute of Education in Bloomsbury.

* * *

At the beginning, Cathy Avent took me on some of her own visits, where I was able to listen and participate in her discussions with the heads and meet careers teachers and examine the quality of careers materials. All this gave me a useful benchmark for my own future visits to schools. She also invited me to attend the appointment of a careers teacher in a Roman Catholic secondary school. Subject inspectors attended such appointments of heads of departments, as a matter of course. They were expected to challenge any racist or sexist questions asked by the governors, which Cathy had to do on this occasion, when the local priest asked the female candidate questions about who looked after her children when she was working.

It was the inspectors' role to ask technical questions relating to the subject and, at the end, to sum up the qualities and the qualifications of the various candidates. The choice, however, lay with the governors, though they usually paid attention to the advice offered by the inspector.

Once, years later, I had to dissent from the choice governors made when they chose someone relatively inexperienced over a person with huge experience and expertise. They said their preferred candidate 'reminded them of their previous careers teacher'. The distinguished chair of governors, a former leader of the ILEA, was angry, because I did not feel able to endorse the governors' choice. He said he would write to the Chief Inspector. I told him he was entitled to do that and I would also write to the Chief Inspector, which I did. There were no repercussions.

Although I was based at County Hall, I spent much of my time at 377 Clapham Road, where we ran our courses for careers teachers and where the London branch of the NACGT, of which I was a member, met and held its meetings for members. Once the elegant country house of a wealthy family in the early 19th century, it had a friendly, welcoming air. There were pear trees in the back garden, which flowered profusely in the spring, and plenty of shrubs in the front garden, under which a homeless woman, reputedly the former wife of a doctor, often spent the night.

Whenever I pass the building these days, I say to myself: 'Et in Arcadia ego'.

I supervised Avril Hill, the careers advisory teacher; Andrew Buchanan, the advisory teacher for JIIG-CAL worked to David. I also had responsibility for the DISCOS, whose number had increased to 10, so that every ILEA division now had one.

CHAPTER SEVEN

School Industry Initiatives, 1984-6

The new recruits to the DISCO team, who were appointed in April 1984, as a result of the recommendations in *Improving Secondary Schools*, were as talented and highly motivated as the first wave had been. They came from a variety of backgrounds but many had some industrial experience as well as teaching qualifications. At my urging, the ILEA negotiated with the Schools' Council Industry Project to include all 10 of them in the SCIP network. As part of their induction, the DISCOs were sent on a consultancy course organised by British Gas, which gave them the skills to work with teachers and industrialists.

I encouraged them to write regular reports of their work and send copies to their own divisional inspector and also to David Chambers or me. When we received one, David and I made it a priority to meet the DISCO and the divisional inspector. We did this for two reasons. We wanted to raise the profile of schools industry work, in the divisions, and also to assess what support the DISCO had. These visits also informed us about the local economy and the nature of the schools and colleges in that area.

DISCOs publicised their work by writing articles in ILEA's

newspaper, *Contact,* or in *SCIP News* as well as local newspapers and journals, in order to spread the knowledge of school industry initiatives across the ILEA and elsewhere. Certain common threads emerged from these descriptions of work in secondary, primary and special schools, even in areas with different socio-economic profiles.

Acting as interpreters between schools, industry and business, the DISCOs arranged for pupils and teachers to go out into the world of work and invited people from trade unions, business and industry into the schools. They were responsible for ensuring that both teachers and industrialists were carefully briefed about their tasks as were the pupils who were engaged in mini-enterprises or simulations or other activities. At the end, the DISCOs also carried out an evaluation of the whole process in order to draw out the learning from it.[56]

One of the new recruits to the DISCO team was Peter Holdsworth, based in Greenwich. He worked in commerce for four years before training as a teacher. Originally a drama specialist, he had taught English and Careers Education. He was then a careers advisory teacher for a year, with Cathy Avent and David Chambers.

In 1986, after the new DISCOs had been in post for 18

---

[56] Sean Lawlor and Farquhar McKay produced manuals to guide teachers, pupils and schools through these processes.

months, Peter made a collection of articles they had written and published in various newspapers and journals. They were put together by Connie Godfrey in Division 6, Greenwich, and produced at the Gordon Teachers' Centre as a booklet entitled *Schools Industry Initiatives* (c1986).The first article was by Peter himself on 'The Role of a Disco:'[57]

> 'Working as a DISCO does have its problems,' he wrote. 'First there's the title...Still, it does have the advantage of being easily remembered... The DISCO brief is very wide and our role in many ways unusual. We work for all the schools in our "patch" – secondary, special and primary- and are not confined to any subject areas...
>
> 'The work is concerned with facilitating curriculum development ... designed to promote and understanding of industrial society... and the local community. We always work alongside individual teachers, planning, resourcing and evaluating ... the curriculum. These [developments] might range from a complete sixth form course on "Understanding Industry" to two short sessions on trades unions for a fifth year class or even a project on the theme of "Work" for a primary school. The final and often most important of this developmental process is the involvement of people and expertise from local industry and the

[57]It was originally published in *Newscheck*, Vol 2 No 12, July 1985

community.'

The other articles in *Schools Industry Initiatives* illustrated the range of work done by the DISCOs. George Scudamore, the DISCO for Southwark, had worked in industry before turning to teaching. He taught Art and English, had been Youth Tutor and Head of Community Studies in Wakefield and then Youth Tutor and Head of Adult Education in Redbridge.

George set up a link between Geoffrey Chaucer School and Otis Elevators Plc in Stockwell which resulted in 'The Lifts Project.' This was described in the second article in *School Industry Initiatives,*[58] by Peter Vaughan, head of physics and electronics at Geoffrey Chaucer:

> 'Pupils were about to start on the 'electronic logic' section of their course. We decided to embark on a project to make a working model of a lift... Electronic logic is all about making circuits perform various switching operations in the right order at the right time, which is precisely what happens in a modern lift installation. In selecting 15 pupils, a deliberate attempt was made to include pupils across the entire range of ability... We were also keen to see how the pupils would respond to the responsibility of being part of a team... A meeting with Mr John James, Personnel and Training Officer at Otis, proved valuable in clearing up

---

[58] *School Industry Initiatives pp5-6*

certain technical points as well as in planning the on-site visits for the pupils.

'Each pupil was given a design project appropriate to their ability. Some... were made responsible for the overall system... others were charged with ... testing procedures. The aim was to adopt, as realistically as possible the approach of an industrial design team, necessitating close co-operation and individual responsibility.

'On-site visits took place four weeks into the project. Otis arranged for us to inspect their installations at a building in the West End. This provided the opportunity to see how the various design problems had been solved in real life and to obtain the definitive answer to the question "What happens if the rope breaks?" Otis were extremely generous in providing two of their senior engineers for the two afternoons of the visits, who acted as instructors and guides, answering questions patiently and allowing pupils to peer at the bits you normally prefer not to think about, like the emergency hand winding gear.

'The pupils responded enthusiastically to the challenges and have a better understanding of electronic logic than previous classes... It also gave me the opportunity to appreciate more fully the types of skills and abilities required of school leavers by industry.'

* * *

Jenny Edwards described the mini-enterprises run by fourth year pupils at Southfields and Garratt Green Schools in Wandsworth.[59] Both schools suspended their normal timetables near the end of the summer term.

> 'By day one of the fortnight, Garratt Green had seven mini-enterprises and Southfields had 14. Before the pupils could get a loan of money, they had to convince a team of local business people and teachers that their idea was workable and that they had done sufficient research and planning…'

Despite this, not all was plain sailing for those involved in the Odd Jobs/ Gardening Mini-Enterprise.

> 'Four pupils decided that people in the area might need some to do their odd jobs and gardening. They found the pricing of jobs was difficult… The work was exhausting but satisfying. "The problems of the jobs were easily overcome but the problems within the group were worse and could not be ironed over." One of the group felt a solution might have been to "have made rigid rules for the governing of each enterprise to allow everyone to have a say in the running, which would have prevented dominant personalities taking over."…

---

[59] Jenny Edwards' article, from which these extracts are taken was originally published in *View,* the DTI magazine in Spring 1984, and later reprinted in *School Industry Initiatives*

> 'One of the T-shirt groups secured a large order with a down-payment by impressing their customer with a high-quality sample. But they had not anticipated that their supplier might not have ... 100 yellow T-shirts. Initially, they were very depressed and worried at letting down their customer. Eventually, they found a supplier and were able to complete the order. "Our customers were pleased when they saw the T-shirts ... We worked hard to get all the T-shirts well printed and not smeared. If we did it again, we would get the orders all sorted and work out how much time is needed. We'd check our suppliers and make sure we had plenty of help and not be rushed off our feet."
>
> 'On winding up their enterprises, [all the pupils involved] audited the books carefully. During the next couple of days they spent time, individually, in their groups and with interested visitors, reflecting on... what they had learnt from their successes and mistakes.'

* * *

Mick Shew, who trained as a physics teacher and taught science for 10 years in three London schools, was appointed as, DISCO for Islington, Division 3. 'Developing an Urban Studies Pack,' [60] was an example of one of his projects:

---

[60] *School Industry Initiatives,* p19

'Lack of parks and play areas is a particular problem in Islington, where there is less open space per head of population than any other Borough. Young people frequently have to cross major roads to gain access to play space. The Islington Geography Forum… [worked] with Pat Collarbone, Geography Advisory Teacher, and myself. [T]hey invited members of the Islington Planning department to a meeting to discuss developing an urban studies project based on "Open Space in Islington." The idea was to produce a pack of materials that would enable students to look at the problem, study ways in which new parks had been developed in the past and encourage them to become involved in decisions that affect their environment in the future.

'The planning department not only provided resources such as surveys, maps, etc., but spent time discussing various ideas in the group. The project was divided into three parts: "Availability of Open Space", "Searching for Open Space," and "Planning an Open Space." The first and third parts are now complete. ' "Planning an Open Space" is based on a development at "Gillespie Park" in Highbury district and involves pupils not only in planning a park for themselves, but in the simulation of a public meeting to decide the siting of a proposed park. Gillespie Park was itself developed as a result of consultation with local people. "Searching for Open Space" is a board game of the snakes and ladders type. It represents the problems involved in finding areas of land to use as Open Space, and is being produced by the Isledon Teachers' centre at the moment after a successful trial at Holloway School.'

* * *

Farquhar McKay and Sean Lawlor, working as DISCOs in Hackney and Tower Hamlets, respectively, ran a course in Divisions 4 and 5 on *'Teaching about Unemployment.'*[61] Sixteen teachers and almost as many AOTs (Adults Other Than Teachers) attended some or all of the five weekly sessions.

It was planned in discussion with community groups dealing with unemployment counselling. The course provided the opportunity for teachers to meet people in the wider community involved with the increasing number of young school leavers, facing unemployment. The sessions involved as much practical activity and discussion as possible.

'Session 1: Survival' – a simulation, developed by Community Service Volunteers, put players into situations, forcing them to understand the problems of the young unemployed. Discussion dealt with ways of dealing with bureaucracies and providing counselling.

'Session 2: A group task session involving discussion of the

[61] *School Industry Initiatives pp18-19*

following questions:

What should pupils know about unemployment? What attitudes do young people need to acquire to deal with unemployment? What attitudes should teachers encourage in young people towards employment and unemployment?

'Session 3: A Political Education Advisory Teacher[62] analysed the various causes of unemployment and demonstrated the use of a game 'Can You Get The Job?' which helps young people to build up a profile explaining why some people get jobs and others don't.

'Session 4: Time to Spare'. Careers teachers from a local college of further education discussed ways in which they approached unemployment as part of a course designed for a mixed ability group.

'Session 5: The group watched 'Rights –Wot Rights?' a video produced by Birmingham Trades Union Research Centre, and discussed some of the implications of YTS for young people.

'One of our aims in organising this course,' Farquhar wrote, 'was to plan modules of work we can put into practice in our own schools. In the event, while we considered ways in which we

[62] I believe this was Julia Fiehn

could adapt some of the activities we used to a local situation, no original, locally based materials were produced. However, we hope that those teachers and AOTs who attended gained helpful insights into the most difficult question of how to talk to young people about unemployment.'

*   *   *

On 23 May 1986, ILEA's *Contact* newspaper ran a double page spread of articles on the DISCOs which illustrated the diversity of the DISCOs' work. It featured the work of Barbara Carter in Division 1, and Jill Key in Division 7.

During a year's secondment to Hatfield Polytechnic, Barbara Carter had taken part in a CBI 'Teachers into Industry Scheme'. She was then appointed lecturer in charge of careers at Southwark College, before becoming a DISCO in Kensington and Chelsea. Barbara worked with the English department in Fulham Cross Girls' School to design an eight lesson module on trades unions. The planning group brainstormed the issues which faced trades unions locally and nationally and, as Fulham Cross was a multi-ethnic girls' school, decided to include women's rights and race.

> 'A simulation on the privatisation of domestic services in a hospital took up … two lessons. It was a local issue and raised questions such as pay, working conditions, health and safety, job security and pension and maternity rights…The pupils… assumed the roles of domestics,

> nurses, doctors, NUPE[63], management and the District Health Authority (DHA). They worked in small groups and many of them met after school or telephoned each other at home to prepare their cases for the DHA meeting. One girl, who has steadfastly refused to take up a pen in English lessons for months, returned the next day with one and half pages of writing which could not be faulted by her teacher. She had spent the evening discussing the issues with her mother.
>
> 'From there, we moved on to an industrial relations role play on racial abuse at work. The personnel manager of a large local firm attended a lesson and thought it a great success. Next we showed a video and then worked in small groups to discuss issues for women at work. Each group produced a flipchart of a "Working Women's Charter" and presented it to the class. The women unionists present joined in the group discussions and led the debriefing sessions… one girl remarked: "It was … more grown up, than a lot of the things we do."[64]

Another of Barbara's projects resulted in a video, *Design for Living,* which highlighted the wide-ranging career opportunities in design. Made for Division 1's Education and Industry Partnership,

---

[63] The National Union of Public Employees represented public sector workers (1908-1993)
[64] Article by Barbara Carter in *ILEA Contact* 23 May 1986

which Barbara founded, it was produced by the ILEA's Television and Publishing Centre and was sponsored by 16 design firms. The video was launched at Pentagram, one of Europe's leading design companies. I was delighted when Barbara invited me to attend the ceremony.

*　　*　　*

The impact of the recession on the local economy in Lewisham posed real problems for Jill Key, who had been appointed there, in the 1982. However, she did not let that stop her.

> 'Sainsbury's new Superstore in Lee Green might seem an unlikely starting point for developing the curriculum. But that is exactly what happened as part of Division 7's Teachers into Industry Scheme. Geography teacher, Roger Lawrence, spent two weeks … in Lewisham's planning department and saw the teaching implications which lay behind Sainsbury's proposals… Because Roger had built up such a good relationship with the planners, he was allowed access to many of the papers involved in the application. And Sainsbury's, too, were willing to co-operate when the local Division 7 Geography Forum expanded Roger's ideas into a teaching pack.'

> 'The Teachers into Industry Scheme allowed teachers in the Division to spend time with a local commercial organisation as part of a school based in-service exercise… Local firms in Lewisham are involved in the project and

have expressed interest and commitment to establishing links with local schools... General aims for all teacher secondments have been identified. It is expected that any teacher spending time with an organisation will increase the dialogue and mutual understanding between local schools and local industry. The teacher should come away from the placement with an accumulation of information which could be used in lessons and ideas and contacts for using the local economic community as a teaching resource.'[65]

> 'A computer studies teacher who spent a week with Lewisham's computer services department… has now built close links between his school and the department. Science teachers who visited Sainsbury's laboratories are adapting tests to complement the mainstream teaching such as testing the amount of chalk in toothpaste and acids in our food and what exactly goes in to our cleaning materials.'[66]

In a recent email to me, Jill described how she also arranged for a textiles teacher, Sally Herbert, to spend time in a local dress factory and a week with Marks and Spencer:

> '[Sally] visited a clothing factory off the Old Kent Road. A fascinating placement where she, and I, learnt the importance of the over-locking machine in making clothes

[65] Article by Jill Key in *School Industry Initiatives*.p20
[66] Article by Jill Key in *ILEA Contact* 23 May 1986

and also how the profit for the company came not from the contract for the manufacturing but from the skill of the cutter who managed, by his expertise, to cut more garments from the cloth[67] so the company could sell the extras via other outlets, mainly market stalls I suspect. I would imagine that is long gone, with computer design ensuring the maximum use of the cloth.

'Another interesting fact that came from this placement were the standards for the workshop and care of the employees expected by Marks and Spencer. At the time of this placement M&S were proudly claiming that their clothes were all manufactured in the UK.[68] I wonder if these standards still apply for M&S and other companies, especially from the overseas factories in the light of the horrific fires and building collapses?

'A second placement was to Marks and Spencer, Lewisham branch. I think this was a Maths teacher as the thing that sticks in my mind was the importance of the number 12 for deliveries and packaging. 12 can be divided into 3 x 4 and 6 x 2 unlike 10 which can only be 5 x 2. 3 x4 was a much better grouping for packaging and display.'

---

[67] See below where 'coupage' is also mentioned in Mary Harris's project '*Maths in Work*' p 132

[68] Email to Anne Dart Taylor from Jill Clarke nee Key 29.10.2004

CHAPTER EIGHT

Storm Clouds over the ILEA 1984-87

The political climate in which we were working began to change. In 1983 the government published a white paper, which set out the case for abolishing the Greater London Council.[69] The Local Government Act of 1985 was passed in Parliament by a narrow majority and on 31st March 1986 the GLC ceased to exist. Its assets were assigned to the London Residuary Body.

The possibility of abolishing the ILEA, which was a special committee of the GLC, at the same time, was discussed. However, many people, including Dr Tessa Blackstone,[70] then Deputy Education Officer for the ILEA, argued that the boroughs were not yet ready to take on education, so the ILEA was allowed to continue as a directly elected body but now it was rate-capped by the Government.

Frances Morrell won the Islington South and Finsbury seat in the elections of 1987 but was deposed as leader of the ILEA by

---

[69] Ironically the Paving Bill was drawn up by a friend of our family, a senior civil servant, who lived in Wimbledon.

[70] In 1987 she was made a life peer as Baroness Blackstone of Stoke Newington. She sits on the Labour benches.

the more circumspect Neil Fletcher. He continued to support the policy of using the inspectorate to improve secondary schools. Indeed he was committed to giving parents more information about how schools were performing. Documents, such as *Keeping the School Under Review,* enabled schools to check on their own performance.

Neil Fletcher also courageously began to tackle the problem which Frances Morrell had ducked. The number of children of school age was dropping in certain boroughs but rising in others. As a result, some schools had surplus teachers, while others were understaffed. The radical Inner London Teachers Association objected to the necessary redeployment but the presence of some teachers with no timetable hanging around the staff room created ill-feeling in those overstaffed schools. It was high time it was tackled.

*　　　*　　　*

There were also changes within our careers team. To my great sadness, Cathy Avent was due to retire in November 1984, just six months after I joined the Inspectorate.[71] Her post was advertised nationally not as Senior Inspector for Careers Education but as a Staff Inspector's job. It was ironic that Cathy, who had created the job and had done it so brilliantly that it was now upgraded, had never been given that title herself but had been designated Senior

---

[71] She has remained a dear friend to this day.

Inspector. She encouraged both David Chambers and me to apply. I did so, without any expectation of getting the job, as I was still a novice.

David, however, had a longer track record in the Inspectorate. He was widely respected and much loved in the ILEA. I hoped he would be appointed but there was tough competition from Peter Heaviside, who was the Chief Careers Officer in Brent, and Graham Elliot, a Careers Adviser from Sheffield. The appointment was sufficiently senior to be made by ILEA Elected Members. I remember we four candidates were asked to wait in one of the magnificent panelled rooms of County Hall.[72] I was extremely nervous during my interview and thought some of the Members seemed negative.

Afterwards, we were kept waiting for what seemed like ages. Finally, Graham Elliot was called back, to be offered the job. David, Peter and I knew little about him but we hoped that he would be good - and would be able to fill Cathy's shoes. The three of us went downstairs to the restaurant where we had a coffee together and commiserated with one another.

It was perhaps a fortnight before we heard that Graham Elliot had turned down the job because his family didn't want to leave Sheffield. The Chief Inspector, Dr Hargreaves, was furious.

---

[72] This glorious building now houses two hotels, an aquarium and some exclusive flats.

He summoned David Chambers to his office in County Hall, told him the news and said that he was to be the Acting Staff Inspector for careers education and guidance. There was no suggestion that the substantive post should be re-advertised[73]. Nor was an acting inspector appointed to bring the team up to its full strength. By first accepting the job, when it was offered to him, and then refusing it, Graham Elliott did us a great disservice.

He returned to his former job. National Association of Careers & Guidance Teachers (NACGT) colleagues of mine, working in Sheffield told me he was good at it. Peter Heaviside had a distinguished record in the Careers Service and ended up as head of it, in the Department for Trade and Industry.[74]

* * *

David and I had to soldier on, in the ILEA, with two inspectors instead of three, covering the 144 secondary schools, 17 colleges of further education not to mention the innumerable off site units, and special schools. We did at least have two advisory teachers, Andrew Buchanan, the JIIG-CAL co-ordinator, and Avril Hill[75],

---

[73] I suspect David Chambers was Dr Hargreaves preferred choice but he was overruled by Members . When Graham Elliott withdrew, Dr Hargreaves decided not to put David through the ordeal of another interview but keep him as an Acting SI.

[74] In the 1990s, when I was working in Doncaster, I ran a NACGT conference there. Peter Heaviside came, in attendance on the Minister, Ann Widdecombe, our main speaker. I remember he told me she was an excellent. hard working Minister.

[75] Years later, after the abolition of the ILEA, I was in London for a meeting of the Guidance Council and ran into Avril Hill on a platform of the Underground.

for careers education and guidance in schools.

David transferred to County Hall and I moved to Clapham. The move suited me well, not least, because it meant I had a much shorter journey to work and the atmosphere was more informal. I'm not sure David enjoyed County Hall as much. At Clapham, I shared an office on the first floor, with Yvonne Beecham, inspector for social sciences, who became a good friend. I remember that she and I did the ILEA's ground breaking anti-racism course together. I suspect we were stroppy course members, as we both felt our equal opportunities awareness was high. In my case, my M. Phil had been a study of racism in history textbooks.

Despite this, I found the course helpful and I was better prepared to assist in the investigation of a case of racial discrimination. A black female deputy head applied for the post of head teacher in the school where she worked. She was not appointed and appealed against the decision.

Maureen Walshe, the immensely experienced Staff Inspector for home economics, whose teachers' centre was next to ours in Clapham, led the investigation. She asked Mike Hussey, the Zimbabwean head of the multi-ethnic and anti-racist education team, and me to join her. It was a difficult assignment but I

She recognised me by the turquoise suit I was wearing, which I had put on that morning for the first time in years. Avril was at a critical point in her career, so we sat and discussed that as if we were still members of the same team.

enjoyed working with Maureen and Mike and learnt a great deal from them. In the end, we upheld the deputy head's complaint.

* * *

In 1985-6, David Chambers carried out a survey of careers education and guidance in further education colleges, which identified the need for a specialist advisory teacher for that sector. Traditionally, our team had been involved only with secondary schools. However, as a DISCO, I had worked with the colleges in Division 2 and had discovered that the provision of careers education there was patchy and variable in quality, so I supported David's initiative with enthusiasm. Our first further education advisory teacher, Judy Early, was appointed in December 1986 and worked with the team from 1987-1989. It was a tough assignment, as Judy told me recently: [76]

> 'The one thing I do remember is learning a huge amount from Kay, Peter and yourself, Anne, about the good practices used in careers education in secondary schools which helped me in supporting FE teachers. Having said that, it was quite a struggle to convince some of the FE staff, in London colleges, to change their thinking with students, [and become] the "guide on the side", as opposed to the "sage on the stage." However, I like to think I played

[76] Judy, who now uses her maiden name Woolfe, sent these comments to me in an email 21.09.2014

a small part in changing attitudes and practices in many of the colleges towards more student-centred approaches.

> 'I was grateful for the advisory role as it equipped me with amazing skills which were very useful in my future work - especially at City University (1995-2008) where I set up an academic learning support scheme for mature students. In the early stages, most of the work involved negotiating with tutors and senior management about resources and training etc. As far as I'm aware the scheme is now embedded in the university and is used by hundreds of students.'

Judy's major contribution to our work was developing a tape/slide show to help careers teachers and lecturers to set up a careers room, which I refer to below.[77] Judy's advent was welcome not least because David's work load and mine was growing. Dr Hargreaves, who had been recruited by Frances Morrell with the intention of raising standards, asked inspectors to make 'substantial' school visits, including viewing lessons, and increased the number of full inspections of ILEA schools.

On my visits, I had already experienced how the quality of schools varied. Where the leadership was inadequate, standards of behaviour and teaching suffered. I remember parking my car outside one mixed school at lunch time and eating a sandwich. Suddenly a boy vaulted over the wall and ran off up the road. It

[77] see below p238

was clearly not the first time he played hookey. He vanished before I could do anything about it.

There were some boys' schools which I went into, with a strongly macho ethos, where I felt distinctly uncomfortable. By contrast, in a much sought after church school for boys, in Kensington, the pupils were courteous. There, I was critical of the lack of careers education below sixth form level, because the school assumed that everyone would stay on into the sixth form and did not offer alternative pathways. After a brisk discussion with the Head and careers teacher about my concerns, I was whisked into the Chapel for Compline.

In a girls' school, in Peckham, I noticed with astonishment that the cloakroom was unlocked even though pupils' bags were hanging up there. Most school children carried their bags, full of textbooks, exercise books and PE kit, with them everywhere, cluttering the classrooms during lessons. In some schools, they could be persuaded to leave them in lockers but in an open cloakroom? I questioned the head about it.

'My dear,' she said to me, 'this is a church school.'

A mixed church school, in Peckham, was attended by the children of a West African colleague of my husband. The children were well integrated and flourished in the calm atmosphere.

There were also outstanding community schools, which I came to know well, including a boys' school in Tooting, which was tough but purposeful. The careers department was well resourced and staffed, commanding respect from staff and pupils. The head of careers told me about a lad who rejected all the advice about training courses, which he was given, because he was determined to become a snooker player. 'You won't be able to make a career out of that,' said his careers teacher, but Jimmy White managed to do so. Similarly, in other schools, in Vauxhall, Holland Park, Hampstead, and Camden, excellent management and good teaching ensured a safe environment and a good all-round education.

* * *

In an attempt to provide all the Authority's schools with a balanced intake, from 1972 onwards, all London pupils were assessed by head teachers, at the end of their primary schooling, given a Verbal Reasoning Test (VRT) and put into three bands. Twenty five percent of children were deemed to be 'above average' and were allocated to Band One; 50% were deemed to be 'average' and were put in Band Two; the remaining 25% in Band Three were classified as 'below average'. The results of the VRT, which was a group rather than an individual test, enabled the head teacher to adjust the distribution of numbers in each band in the proportion that they were found in local primary schools. It was replaced in

1987 by the more objective London Reading Test.[78]

Secondary schools were obliged to take pupils from all three bands, so that there was a fair distribution of places across the Authority. This system was the exact opposite of the parental choice system more commonly used today. Even in the 1980s, some enterprising parents selected a secondary school outside their immediate area. For example, I was aware of a number of pupils from the Brixton area who travelled by underground to schools north of the river, which had a better reputation than some of their local schools.

The 'failing' schools were often located in areas of social deprivation and high unemployment, where there were few prospects for school leavers, but good leadership and management always had a beneficial effect on the ethos and quality of schooling provided.

* * *

Taking part in whole school inspections brought me into contact with long-serving, experienced colleagues, from diverse backgrounds and different areas of the ILEA. I enjoyed collaborating with them and learnt a great deal about the nature and conduct of inspections from them. Some had been head teachers, some heads of department in a large school. Many were

---

[78] Anne West & Hazel Pennel in *Choice and Diversity in Schooling; Perspectives and* Prospects ; ed Carl Bagley; Ron Glatter, Philip Woods; Routledge 27 Jun 2005

subject inspectors, as I was, or from specialist teams, such as the multi-ethnic one.

There were also district and divisional inspectors who had oversight of a number of schools. Each brought his or her individual focus to the inspection. We were aided in our inspections by information on the schools' performance from ILEA's highly respected Research and Statistics Branch, led by Peter Mortimore and his successor, Desmond Nuttall.

Cathy Avent had talked to me about taking part in inspections, during my induction. However, when Dr Hargreaves became Chief Inspector, the number of inspections was increased and they were based on a new template. We used the headings from the document : *Keeping the School Under Review,* namely: the aims of the school or department; its management; curriculum planning; learning experiences; pupil assessment and record keeping and, finally, the relationships beyond the school, with parents, with careers officers, with social services and industry. We were supposed to grade each of the categories on a scale of 1-4.[79] An even number was deliberately chosen to prevent us taking refuge in a mid- way point. We had to give a verdict of outstanding, good, unsatisfactory or poor. Some of these areas were easier to make judgements about than others.

When we received documents in advance of the inspection,

---

[79] This prefigured OFSTED's grades.

it was possible to make initial judgements about how good or bad the aims of the school were and how well planned its curriculum was, though it was still necessary to check that the aims were put into practice and the curriculum plans were actually implemented. However, we had to be in the school building before we could experience the quality of the management. Was the atmosphere of the school orderly and calm? Did the teachers feel well supported by the management? Did they have access to in-service training? Or were they rebellious and downtrodden? What was the behaviour of pupils like in lessons, in the corridors and in the playgrounds? Were they calm, confident, responding well to teachers' advice? Or were they out of control?

The ILEA Research and Statistics Branch provided us with an excellent analysis of grades achieved by pupils in examination results as well as information about the social background of the pupils which might have an impact on those results.

Looking through books during an inspection, we could see the quality or otherwise of pupil assessment and record keeping but we needed to be in a lesson to decide whether any learning was going on and to make a judgement about its quality. Sitting in a classroom, observing a lesson was always instructive. It was easier to talk about the quality of teaching rather than learning. Some experienced teachers coached their pupils for their examinations, telling them the answers which would be acceptable, rather than allowing them to think for themselves. They might be rewarded with good examination results but pupils' imaginations were not fired.

Other teachers challenged their pupils with unexpected questions making them hungry to learn but sometimes a brilliant lesson went over the heads of some or all of the pupils. We needed to discover how the less able were supported? And how were the most able challenged? Often the only differentiation provided was simpler or more difficult worksheets. The quality of the worksheets themselves was frequently dire.

One of the characteristics of the DISCOs' work was the use of active learning, through simulations, or mini-enterprises, so I was always delighted to find classrooms where children were working in small groups, to solve problems themselves and then feeding back their answers in a plenary session. Some of the most able teachers appeared to do very little, except set a task, wander round the classroom, facilitating discussions, and occasionally, when a group had ground to a halt, suggesting a way forward.

One of the most interesting inspections in which I was involved was of an ILEA special boarding school, for boys with educational and behavioural problems. I was so new that I didn't know ILEA had any boarding provision. I was impressed by the provision the staff made in preparing the pupils for the transition to adult life. The school had a flat where two or three boys in their final year lived, learning to keep house and to cook for themselves and how to manage a budget. I was, however, concerned to find that so many of the pupils were Black British. I wondered what was happening in mainstream schools that so alienated these lads?

Another innovative inspection, in Islington, looked specifically at the provision made for talented and gifted children. I talked to a number of the girls and to the careers teacher, in order to discover what advice was given to pupils who were gifted musically, artistically or in dance, as well as those who were academically brilliant. I also examined the records of former pupils' progression from school into higher and further education, looking at which universities they were applying to. The ILEA offered wonderful opportunities in all these areas but I was keen to see them going further afield as well. Muslim girls wanted to apply to single sex colleges, of which my own, St Hilda's, was still one.

A third inspection, in Wandsworth, was personally interesting because the Head there had been Head of Paddington and Maida Vale High School, when I was first teaching in London. She had married, so when I read her name in the ILEA Green Book[80] it meant nothing to me. I don't know which of us was more surprised when I turned up as part of the general inspection team. However, relations were friendly, despite the fact that our situations had been reversed. The school was as well-managed as P.M.V.H.S. had been, though I judged the careers department to be under resourced.

---

[80] The Green Book was our indispensable directory of schools and personnel.

These full inspections and the subsequent reports, which we had to write, took up a lot of time. We relied heavily on the advisory teachers, Andrew Buchanan, Avril Hill and Judy Early to visit schools and colleges to support newly appointed staff and to alert us if there were any problems with careers departments, which required an inspector's visit.

With Cathy's Avent's retirement, David and I also had to share out attendance at governors' interviews for candidates for careers teacher posts. These always took place in the evening because many governors were working during the day. One night, I was expected at Tulse Hill, a school I had not visited before. The Brixton riots were still vivid in my memory. I lost my way and stopped to ask a black couple who were walking down the road. I remember the man smiled broadly as he gave me the directions and told me he was a former pupil. Another night, my car's battery failed. I managed to park it somewhere near a pub, from where I rang and asked Humphrey to come and tow me home.

* * *

I imagine the increased workload and pressure weighed particularly heavily on David Chambers, our Acting Staff Inspector. Like many people at the time, David smoked but, unusually, he always rolled his own cigarettes.[81]. My memory of

---

[81] I had given up smoking after we returned to the UK from Malawi, where tobacco was grown and 200 cigarettes cost the equivalent of 50p

him is sitting on one of the low chairs in the Careers Education and Resources Centre (CERC), opening a tin, taking out a cigarette paper, filling it with strands of tobacco, rolling it up, and licking the paper to stick it together, and then lighting the resulting weedy cigarette.

David was a calming influence on me, in those first few frenetic months in the Inspectorate. He continued my induction by taking me with him to meet Mrs. Pat Smith, the Chief Careers Officer, and her senior colleagues at the Careers Service headquarters. These regular meetings were always fruitful and our partnership was a close one, as indeed it needed to be. We discussed particular schools, which concerned us because of the quality of careers education and advice provided.

It was helpful for us to have the view-point of careers officers who went into ILEA schools and colleges, to interview pupils and students at transition points. They worked closely with our careers teachers in schools and colleges and collaborated with them in organising careers conventions. One careers officer had the job of going round all the schools and weeding out from the shelves and cabinets any information which was out of date, an absolutely vital job if pupils were to be given accurate advice.

Many careers officers were members of the London branch of the National Association of Careers Teachers (NACGT), with which I became involved. Tony Evans, co-ordinator for 16-19 education in Greenwich, suggested I should stand for election to the National Council in 1986, which I did and was duly elected. Tony, then the President of the Council, drove me to the Council Meetings in Stoke Rochford, a teacher training college. The main building was beautiful but the students' accommodation was bleak and we had to trail down long corridors to the shower and bathrooms.

When Tony's Vice Chair, Nikki Sims became President in 1989, she chose me as her Vice President and eventual successor, in 1991. Officers' meetings, which were always lively and intense, were held in one of the staff rooms in the Oxford Street branch of Marks and Spencers in London and followed, in the evening by a dinner at the Gay Hussar in Soho.

Membership of the NACGT brought me into contact with careers teachers and officers across the country, and gave me a national perspective on the provision of careers education and guidance. Through it, I met Tony Watts and Bill Law of the National Institute of Careers Education and Counselling (NICEC) and David Cleaton, Head of Careers in Sussex, who produced the NACGT's *National Survey of Careers Education and Guidance* in 1987.

CHAPTER NINE

Inspectors' Conferences & Special Projects, 1985-7

I went with David Chambers to meetings of the ILEA Inspectorate, called by Dr Hargreaves. These were large, attended by over 100 inspectors, who came from all phases of education, from primary and special schools, through secondary to the further and higher education team, who had their own chief inspector. They included a new category of inspector, introduced by Dr Hargreaves – the IBIS team of Inspectors Based In Schools. Mostly former heads, they were sent into schools which were failing or which had particular problems. The Staff Inspector for the IBIS team was Valerie Jennings, whom I had known as the Head of Haverstock School, when I was a DISCO.

Our meetings often took place at one of the ILEA colleges of further education, which like Westminster, ran catering courses. An excellent lunch was cooked by the students, who also waited on us and served us glasses of wine. Sometimes the afternoon sessions were a little drowsy. Perhaps it was to counteract this that Dr Hargreaves invited various groups to lead in-service training sessions, at the conferences.

At one meeting, the programme was designed and run by

the Women Inspectors' Group (WIGS) to raise equality issues. We had a lot of fun planning it. We decided to do a role play about sizism, though our actual target was discrimination against women. Under the direction of the drama inspector, who was herself vertically challenged, we acted out a number of comic situations, scripted and directed by her, in which she was discriminated against. It caused a lot of laughter.

Afterwards we broke into groups and each woman inspector had to lead a discussion based on statistics about the gender balance in the ILEA Inspectorate. These had been collected and analysed by a woman maths inspector. Surprisingly, given the emphasis the ILEA put on equal opportunities, they showed that men were predominant in the senior posts, for example, Divisional and Staff Inspectors; and women in the junior ones, the District and General Inspectors. By chance, I had the Chief Inspector himself, in my group. As we began to talk about the analysis, Dr Hargreaves said with dawning horror: 'Are you saying that the ILEA Inspectorate is sexist?'

Pointing to the statistics, I nervously suggested it was a possibility, if not at the present, at least historically.

* * *

Despite this, Dr Hargreaves, who had always supported the work of the DISCOs, asked me to invite them to run a number of simulations at an inspectors' conference on 12th September 1986, in County Hall itself. When I approached the DISCOs, they were enthusiastic and felt it was an opportunity not to be missed. We planned the programme together and the DISCOs asked me to give a brief over-view of their work, at the beginning.

The prospect made me acutely nervous. I had only been in the Inspectorate for two years and addressing my experienced and highly qualified seniors, was infinitely more terrifying than talking to a crowded hall full of business men. I comforted myself with the thought that at least the Divisional Inspectors were already aware of the DISCOs' work. Also, a number of subject inspectors, such as Design and Technology, Geography, Science, Art and Textiles had worked with them and were sympathetic.

On arrival, at County Hall, the inspectors were given a hand-out. I then made a brief speech on the role and activities of the DISCO team, describing the Schools Council Industry Project's characteristics of active learning, which could be used right across the curriculum and, indeed, with all age groups, together with the involvement of adults others than teachers, particularly those from business and industry. The inspectors were then divided into seven groups, which were given a briefing, specific to the simulation they were going to undertake.

There is insufficient space here to describe all seven simulations. I will just mention two. One concerned the future of the Stoke Newington Reservoirs. The reservoirs had been used as filters, to purify London's water, and had become a unique inner city nature reserve, where wild plants flourished and rare birds nested. Unfortunately, they were about to made redundant as the Thames Water Board was building a water ring main around the capital and planned to drain the land and sell it for around £50,000,000.

The simulation was developed by Farquhar McKay, the DISCO for Hackney, and Gillian Woodward,[82] who, at that stage, had been seconded from Skinners' Girls' School in Hackney to work with unemployed school leavers. Farquhar and Gillian involved Peter and Elaine Gosnell, co-secretaries of the campaign to save the reservoirs.

Originally, the simulation was part of a three and a half days' induction programme for CPVE students. However, only two hours were available at the Inspectors' Conference so Gillian and Farquhar decided to run the Public Inquiry section of the simulation on its own. The timing was something like this: 2.15-2.20p.m. Introduction; 2.20-3.00p.m. Preparation and submissions; 3.00-3.15p.m. Tea break; 3.15-3.40p.m. Recommendations and comments by the Inquiry Panel; 3.40-4.00p.m. Debriefing, in and out of role.

They invited Peter and Elaine Gosnell to come along as consultants. Farquhar and Gillian gave a brief explanation of the purpose of the exercise. The first aim was to enable inspectors to experience active learning which they could encourage in their

---

[82] Later Gillian took over Jenny Edwards' post as DISCO in Wandsworth

own subject areas. The second was to understand which learning skills were being developed. The third was to assess the quality of this approach to learning.

The participants broke into smaller groups and took on roles as members of the Inquiry Panel; the Press, and Hackney Council, which had to gather information from other groups. Peter Gosnell spoke briefly about the background to the issue, historical and environmental. Each mini-group was given a copy of a *Times* article about the reservoirs and a briefing on their own role, to help them prepare a case to present to the tribunal.

Gillian wrote a case study about the simulation for the SCIP Course, *Industry and Curriculum Change*, in September 1986, which I quote from here:

> 'The groups [of inspectors] set about the task promptly and with considerable animation and the Gosnells were frequently consulted. It was interesting to see people having to take on a persona representing values which were antipathetic to that individual in real life….'
>
> [When they came back after the tea-break], 'each group presented its case with impressive eloquence and wit. The Press was extremely productive and pertinent throughout, with a continuous flow of headlines such as "Toffs Out Say Residents", "No White Highlands", "Drugs, Sex, Aids Fears From Pleasure Palace."…
>
> 'After the Inquiry Panel had issued its stern verdict, we

debriefed firstly with one or more spokespersons from each role giving their feeling "in role". Peter and Elaine Gosnell then described their impressions as experts, remarking on the clarity of the presentations and how near many of them were to what might be happening in real life. Finally...we debriefed in and out of role, with every individual saying something about their feelings about the activity and the value of it. Some interesting comments… were about the discomfort of presenting a case which embodied values contradictory to one's own and some concern about the occasional misuse of simulations about personal issues.

'The inspectors told us that it was a valuable experience, that they hadn't done anything like it before and that the exercise had helped them to go into the benefits and dangers of such an activity… The fact that there were three Hackney residents in the room, which generated extra interest and concern, supported our belief that an issue chosen for study, which directly affects the participants' lives, will work particularly well…One of the inspectors passed the idea on to a member of staff at North London College where the simulation will be run at a later date.'

I didn't join the Reservoirs simulation but instead decided to take part in *Dockopoly*, the planning game about the Docklands re-development, devised by Sean Lawlor, which I had often heard about but had never seen in action. Participants were divided into four groups to decide the future of a dock. The 'developers' had to make sure they made money from the agreed proposals. The 'councillors' had to ensure the needs of the local community were met. The 'local community groups' were there to speak up for their own needs and 'the planners' had to fit the proposals into the strategic plan of the area. As in the simulation run by Gillian and Farquhar, some people had to take on roles which were antipathetic, though personally, I found this instructive.

It was impossible to play this game, modelled closely on the reality in Docklands, without becoming aware of the impact of these changes on local residents. It provoked a vigorous, even heated, discussion among the participants. One inspector became angry, because of the political implications of the simulation. Throwing down his cards, he marched out of the room. In the light of his exit, Sean had to debrief the rest of us with especial thoroughness, both in and out of role, to make sure there were no unresolved issues. He managed it superbly.

The majority of my colleagues, like those engaged in the Reservoirs Simulation, found the exercise absorbing, challenging, and learnt a great deal from it, not only about Docklands area but about active learning and the role of the DISCOs. I hoped that as a result of the Conference, the DISCOs' profile would be raised, their skills appreciated, and that they would be seen as a resource by more subject inspectors and used more widely across the curriculum.

*　　　*　　　*

Besides the full inspectors' conferences, I also attended a number of smaller inspectorate committees, such as the Personal, Social and Health Education (PSHE) Committee, which I eventually chaired. There were occasional tensions between health education and personal development, for which Jill Clay was the inspector, and careers education, which was my bailiwick. This reflected the situation in schools where careers teachers and health education teachers often competed for time, space and resources. Health and drugs education had Government funding, which careers education did not. However, our discussions were useful in resolving the tensions and arriving at a mutual understanding.

*　　　*　　　*

In the course of my time in the Inspectorate, I became involved a number of special projects. For instance, Barrie Stead, the ILEA elected member for Fulham, asked me to hold a conference on the Cooperative Movement on 6th December 1986. I asked the DISCOs to run interactive workshops and, in the process, I learnt a significant amount about the history and current practice of co-operation. Sadly, despite widespread publicity, the number of people who gave up their Saturday to attend the conference was disappointing.

Far and away the most interesting and long-lived project was *Maths in Work*. One day, in 1986, I was summoned to the office of the Chief Inspector, Dr Hargreaves. His PA wouldn't tell me what it was about. As I drove to County Hall, I wondered what on earth I had done wrong? Once, when I was due to speak at a schools-business conference, which involved the great and the good, such as Howard Davies, Director General of the CBI and Controller of the Audit Commission, I received a 'phone call saying the Chief Inspector was waiting for a report from me. I rang my P.A. in a panic. She found the draft report on my desk and rushed it over to his office, so I was able to make my speech, after all.

On this occasion, however, my conscience was clear. I had done everything I was supposed to do and hadn't, as far as I could remember, done anything I was *not* supposed to do, such as committing the ILEA to spending funds, which neither the Chief Inspector nor the Elected Members had authorised.

When I knocked on Dr Hargreaves' door and was told to enter, I found him waving a letter at me. My heart sank, thinking that one of the DISCOs, or work experience co-ordinators or careers advisory teachers, for whom I was responsible, had written something intemperate for which I would be held personally accountable.

On the contrary, the letter was from someone I had never heard of, a mathematics advisory teacher, Mary Harris. She was critical of her inspector, who was trying to close down her project, *Maths in Work*, and she did not pull her punches.

As I read it, Dr Hargreaves remarked that it was a very rude letter. He also said he had been deluged by correspondence from people all over the south of England, pleading with him to allow the project to continue. In desperation, he asked if I would take on Mary Harris's line management and 'sort her out.' I wasn't enormously enthusiastic, as I felt I already had my hands full - but one can't refuse a Chief Inspector.

My diary for 1986 records the first visit I made to Mary at ILECC, the ILEA's educational computing centre, at John Ruskin Street, on 8th August, but after that Mary usually came to see me in CERC. She arrived in a van, in which she kept all her materials and which doubled as her peripatetic office.

Mary proved to be one of the most delightful and innovative people I ever met. We immediately established a rapport, which may have owed something to the fact we had both been at the Oxford High School. As Mary mischievously said later, *Maths in Work* was 'saved by an Old Girls' Network.'

Mary described her project '*Maths in Work,*' in an article in the 1985-6 winter edition of *View.* [83]

> '*Maths in Work* started with the data from the *London-into-Work Survey*, a gold mine of what nearly 1,000 young people say they do in their first job... Ask them about the

---

[83] *View* was a magazine prepared with and for the Department of Trade and Industry (DTI) by the Central Office of Information.

> frequency with which they use maths skills… and they say "never." But invite them to talk about practical problems at work and a range of interesting situations is revealed in which mathematics helps to contribute to the solution. The moral of this is if you want to find out about maths in work don't ask about maths, ask about the gremlins…
>
> 'The answer must surely be to try and get the real context back into school. *Maths in Work* has recently produced a pack of materials called *Wrap It Up*, with a lot of help from the packaging industry… [T]he pack says "Go and design/make box/label in the way they do in industry, gremlins and all." Of course the students have to do a lot of measurement; it would be a poor box indeed without it. But they also do a lot of 3D thinking from 2D materials, they interpret diagrams, they have to look at proportion, they make mistakes and get into arguments, they create, but above all they do their measurement for a purpose and to the degree of accuracy needed by the task and its materials.
>
> 'But one small pack is one small drop in an ocean. That teachers of the less academic buy it as fast as the project can produce it is a measure of need but not alas of educational priority, for the project is a single handed one, with minimal funding and has to stop work on new resources because there is such a rush on published ones.'

My meetings with Mary were always exciting because her lively mind generated so many new projects and ideas. Besides *Wrap It Up,* she also produced other learning materials such as *Hazards* which, with help from London Transport, the Post Office and the Department of Transport, included problems about the placing of bus stops, letter boxes and pedestrian crossings.

Mary had plans for something called *Cardboard Engineering* and another to be based on textile activities. Unfortunately, the funding for the engineering project was not forthcoming but a generous and imaginative grant from the Department of Education and Science allowed *Maths in Work* to survive staffing cuts in the ILEA. The project was transferred to the University of London's Institute of Education, which enabled Mary to undertake a year's investigation of textile activities as a resource for learning mathematics. She particularly wanted to research the gender and culture effects in work place mathematics.[84] She christened this new project '*Cabbage Pack.*' The name was derived from a French word 'Coupage' meaning 'cutting,' particularly cutting economically to make more than the expected numbers of garments from a piece of cloth. [85]

As it progressed, I suggested setting up an exhibition of Mary's learning materials, which were works of art in themselves. Mary wrote in her book *Common Threads: Women, Mathematics*

---

[84] *Schools, Maths and Work* edited by Mary Harris, Falmer Press, p287
[85] Mary herself was an excellent needlewoman, making all her own clothes.

and Work:

> 'The idea, suggested by Anne Taylor, a member of the [*Maths in Work*] steering committee, was so fertile that the limitations of lack of time, a complete absence of funding, and no idea of a title, took second place to its pursuit.' [86]

The exhibition opened at the Institute in November 1987 and toured England for two years. The British Council took it over and presented it in 23 countries during 1991-1994 until it wore out. A year later, the Falmer Press published *Schools, Mathematics and Work,* which was edited by Mary

---

[86] *Common Threads* Trentham Books Ltd 1997. I am proud to have a signed copy.

CHAPTER TEN

The Next Generation of DISCOS 1987

As the first DISCOs moved on, they were replaced by equally talented candidates, who explored new aspects of schools-industry work. When Jenny Edwards, left Wandsworth to work in a further education college, she was succeeded, by Gillian Woodward, who chose to work with the most difficult and disadvantaged pupils. In 1987, in an article for *Newscheck*[87], Gillian described a work-shadowing scheme which she organised for a group of bridging course boys[88], at John Archer School in Wandsworth.

> 'It's Tuesday morning, 20 January. Snow and ice are still thick on the ground. Craig is riding on the back of a tractor over Chelsea football ground. Mark is discussing fashion designs with Sandy, Ruis is watching Mike mend a silver ring, Daniel is learning how wood shapes with time, Mark C. is on his way to a flat being decorated in Park Lane, Ian

---

[87] *Newscheck* Vol 5 No 2 November 1987. The article was originally published in *SCIP News 18*

[88] Bridging courses were jointly organised by a school and a local college for pupils who were unlikely to take GCSE. The courses had a strong vocational element.

is watching Manie tune the engine of Paul Newman's car and Trevor is a foot away from a woman having a growth removed from her abdomen.

> 'This scheme was my first major planning commitment in my role as DISCO and SCIP co-ordinator... We had encouraged the boys to choose more exotic placements in order for them to experience things they wouldn't encounter in their every days lives...We tried also to achieve a balanced representation in terms of race and gender. Two of the work guides were women and two were black...
>
> 'In a meeting with Fred MacNicol, the bridging course tutor, along with the Wandsworth Work Experience Co-ordinator, we decided work shadowing would be an appropriate experience for these boys. If nothing else it would provide a useful lead into work experience.'

Gillian explained that the organisers were concerned more with personal development than specific vocational choice. They wanted to provide the boys with a glimpse of the big wide world of work; to increase their awareness of the complexity of structures at work and further each individual's development. Therefore, they actively involved the students in planning and negotiating difficult journeys. They hoped to increase the confidence of the group, by asking them to describe their experiences to fellow pupils and staff. They also intended to use it to contribute to classroom work and skill development.

The preparations were extensive. The boys drew maps of the routes, wrote their CVs and devised 20 questions to have up their sleeves for the work guides. They took part in role plays around possible awkward moments such as arriving late and noted down expectations to be compared with realities in the later debriefing. The scheme was unusual in that it was combined with a photography project undertaken by Dave Lewis, a young, black professional photographer.

> 'On Friday, 16th January the boys visited [their far flung] work places to familiarise themselves with the route and say hello to the work guide and employer. Examples of initiative included stolidly trudging through snow and ice.
>
> 'On Monday, 19th January: Briefing session with the whole group. Photographs were taken. Two of the boys had experienced what they interpreted as racial abuse. Dave was supportive and practical in his approach, quoting from his own experience and …we got some ideas together on how best to deal with further abusive remarks.
>
> 'Tuesday 20th and Wednesday 21st: the boys were out on their placements and were visited and photographed by Dave. Dave's impressions of the way things were going between guide and shadow were a useful part of the evaluation,
>
> 'Thursday 22nd: Processing photos at Wandsworth photo

co-op. Informal, illuminating feedback during activity.

'Friday 23rd: Debriefing in two groups. Setting up the exhibition. The boys designed the layout, captions, etc.'

The evaluation of the project showed that:

'In all cases, the experience had considerable impact. In one or two, there were immediate, unexpected results such as one boy having the possibility of being taken on as an apprentice. And Ruis's design being taken up for weaving... There were spin offs, such as Ian approaching…James Hunt at an event at Battersea Park and informing him he had just been tuning his engine. Mark C.'s [comment] about the painting and decorating workers out on site: "I didn't realise all trades could work together like that… really efficient." Peter…at the electrical shop [said] "I found I was very helpful to other people…learned to approach the manager…joked around a lot." Trevor at the hospital:"I had to be patient, to keep quiet during long periods of surgery… help calm people down."

'There were hassles… and disappointments…But the moments of excitement and interest out-weighed them. There was a year assembly in the school and examination pupils are asking to try [work-shadowing]. The exhibition was shown in the school and way beyond its boundaries.'

* * *

When Jill Key left Lewisham to take up an appointment with TVEI in Croydon[89], Glennys Hughes Jenkins replaced her in Lewisham. Glennys did some ground breaking work in primary schools:[90]

> 'All DISCOS were charged with developing the curriculum in all educational areas, from primary to FE and HE wherever possible. Perhaps the hardest group to convince were the primary schools - what did the world of work have to do with primary children and schools? That attitude has now changed now, of course, and the work DISCOS did in primary schools certainly led the way in this education adventure. The Division 7 Primary Schools and Industry Project was launched in September 1986, and involved eight primary schools.
>
> 'Each school took a different aspect of the world of work, and developed it in their own way. Schools undertook to explore the world of work in local businesses, the hospital, the council and council services, council planning and local construction sites. Some schools decided to… run mini-enterprises within their schools, aided by AOTs (adults other than teachers). The schools worked closely with other professionals from the various "industries", and their advice, assistance and their generosity with their time was

[89] Jill later was appointed head of a school in Kent.
[90] Email from Glennys Hughes Jenkins to Anne Dart Taylor 20.09.2014

invaluable to the projects.

'In the project we were looking to involve staff and primary children in a range of aims and objectives, alongside developing confidence and understanding in the world of work around them - perhaps an understanding of jobs and areas of work they knew nothing about and might even be interested in, in the future.

'We were also interested in promoting investigative and problem solving skills through involvement in a "real" work situation; facilitating active learning; encouraging collaborative work and communication skills; developing maths, language, science, CDT skills in a new and relevant way and promoting equal opportunities.

'[We increased] children's confidence in tackling new situations, involving children in making decisions about their own learning, using local resources, especially people, bringing AOTs into the classroom, and taking children to work places. This enabled children to appreciate the contribution that is made to society by people in different areas of work, inspiring them to consider wider concepts.

'The schools embraced the project, writing letters, interviewing staff, learning to lay bricks, making a mural, creating a new sign for their school, making bread at Sainsbury's, organising a school tuck shop, designing and making a shower mitt, setting up a car wash company.

They made paper and developed a paper shop, learned about concrete, and Health and Safety and much more.

'The children were fully engaged and learning in many different and new ways, relevance being key to drawing them into the work. And they had fun, so much fun! The links established through this project lasted for many years too.'

* * *

In an article in *View*[91], Michael Joyce, my successor in Camden & Westminster, described an initiative by the General Electrical Council (GEC) which invited a group of 22 sixth formers, 75% of them male, drawn from five schools in North West London to their Hirst Research centre in Wembley. They were presented with six case histories from GEC's advanced research programme. The sessions chosen were fibre optics, digital systems, electrical connectors, computer aid design, new semiconductor materials and electrical failure analysis.

'A major part of the time was spent in the laboratories either on equipment demonstrations or, wherever practicable, with students using apparatus to undertake measurements or check readings. One of the students said afterwards: "We liked being amazed, seeing the in-action stuff, so we really got interested."'

---

[91] The Department of Trade and Industry magazine, published in the winter of 1985-6

Michael also wrote about another project in the summer of 1987:

> 'There are no subject specialisms in a DISCO's work and there is a continuing emphasis on helping to deliver 'active learning' so that experience becomes the focus for pupils to gain insights. On the subject of active learning... at the session at the Textile Teachers' Centre ... I talked about market research with GCSE pupils and gave them the chance to try out a practical simulation. Experiential learning is always enhanced if good reflection, or debriefing, is employed following the exercise.
>
> 'As one example of my own work I will mention the summer school entitled Business Ventures, pupils attending this course are grouped into teams and given one week, a limited budget, advice from business experts, to produce a plan for the start-up of a new business making and marketing a novel brand of chocolate chip cookies. In the course of one week, students are able to produce quite amazing results – a tribute to their entrepreneurial flair and organising skills which often lie dormant in the classroom.'[92]

When Michael left to go to Argentina, it took three of his DISCO

---

[92] Michael Joyce: Article in the Textile Teachers' Centre Newsletter, Summer 1987.

colleagues to run this workshop.

*   *   *

Robert Powell had been a Social Sciences and Social Studies teacher, before replacing Kevin Crompton in Division 10, Lambeth. Like Glennys, Robert chose to work with primary aged children. He wrote an article for *SCIP News 13*, describing his work with Kingswood Primary School, in Lambeth, and the dairy industry.

> 'The dairy industry was an obvious choice of focus for a study of industry and the world of work. Pupils could easily connect the products with their own experience. Also the industry provides ample scope for a range of visits and activities to investigate the stages of production from the cow to the supermarket dairy counter. Key aspects of the course programme are a strategy involving activity-based learning; opening the school to the economic community and bringing industry in; and a focus on the organisational structure and human aspects to the world [of] work, as well as the physical processes of production.
>
> 'Work to date has involved the primary class of 29 pupils (aged 9-10 years) in visits to a dairy farm and a milk bottling plant. High spots of the farm visit were a guided tour in a tractor and helping with the milking. This was followed later by the children manufacturing butter and cheese in the classroom.

'An interesting development was a link-up with the neighbouring Norwood Secondary School. This assisted the consolidation of primary/secondary school links. At the same time it made available the secondary school's well equipped home economics department to the primary school for making butter and cheese. Sue Hayes, a food technologist from the National Dairy Council organised and ran the event. Thanks to senior girls from Norwood School, who worked with groups of Kingswood pupils, all went safely and smoothly. As a spin off for Norwood School, the Head of Home Economics has enlisted the services of the National Dairy Council to help with a Food Technology Course planned for next year. Help from the Council and the advice of the Milk Marketing Board has been invaluable.

'Having looked at the theory and practice of dairy production the next step for pupils is to see cheese production on a commercial scale. An in-depth study of a creamery is planned which will involve the children looking at the structure and organisation of the industry, occupational roles and people's feeling about work... Before going out...pupils are conducting a study of their own school as an organisation. This involves pilot interviews with a cross-section of teaching and non-teaching staff about their jobs. These activities have stimulated the production of a wealth of art work, creative writing, number work and language development.'

* * *

DISCOs also worked with special schools. A two-day vocational forum was organised by the London Education Business Partnership Director, George Scudamore[93], together with Gillian Woodward, from the Wandsworth Industry School Partnership, and two teachers, Gerry Turner and Rosemary Morris, from Oak Lodge School, Balham, for profoundly deaf pupils. Seventeen employers took part. Several were from very large organisations such as British Telecom, British Gas, the Post Office; British Rail, Whitbread and Sainsbury's. Sam Gallop, Honorary Chair of Opportunities for the Disabled was also present.

In an article for SCIP News entitled '*Not favours… Just Opportunities*'[94], Gillian set out the forum's aims: to increase the sensitivity of employers to the particular difficulties deaf people face functioning in a work place and gaining entry to it. Deaf students were to be exposed to more people from the "world of work", and so become more familiar with work-place procedures. They might make contacts they could pursue in the future. Her intention was to raise awareness and confidence on both sides through practice in communicating with each other. She hoped the forum might lead to a change in employers' attitudes and improve

---

[93] George Scudamore had been the DISCO for Southwark, before being seconded to the LEBP as Director.
[94] SCIP News 22 Autumn 1988

equality of opportunity for deaf school leavers. She also hoped people would enjoy themselves.

As part of the preparation for the forum, Gillian spent an afternoon raising her own awareness by talking to the Head, Peter Merrifield, observing classes and asking the teachers questions.

> 'Oak Lodge School is a delightful learning environment, cheerful to look at with a buoyant and relaxed feel to it… Because of good working relations, facilities and relationships, problems have become challenges rather than burdens… There is no doubt that most of the students I saw are happy in this learning community.
>
> 'I was struck by complexities which had not occurred to me before, particularly those of access to concepts and subtlety of meaning for deaf children… Every word they know has been taught to them at some stage. It is hard to get courses suitable for the deaf accepted by the various examining boards who do not appear to be very flexible when faced with these delicate issues. One advantage is undoubtedly the small numbers of school leavers at any one time and the school has a remarkable record of placing 100% of them in further education, training or jobs.
>
> 'The first day's activities were …setting the scene and raising awareness. The video made by "Opportunities for the Disabled" demonstrated the practical needs of the interviewee and interviewer…highlighting ways to enable

> the candidate to express her/himself fully with examples of past work, writing questions and answers, exchange of basic sign language, and the support of an interpreter…There were also useful tips such as sitting in a position which gets benefit of the light on the face, how to shape words clearly and so on…
>
> 'Denton, an ex-pupil, presently at Racal Avionics, was taken on after work-experience, which led to permanent employment for him and…two other deaf pupils. He emphasised the need for deaf pupils to push themselves forward, [and] often take the first step in over-coming embarrassment in themselves and other people… Employers described with enthusiasm the rewards of working with deaf people, of the qualities of friendliness and patience and co-operation and the high standards of their work.'

The second day began with an icebreaker. Several mimes were presented by pupils, staff and employers. In one exercise, employers as well as students had to choose a badge depicting a particular job and then mime it. The Deputy Head, Gerry Turner, said:

> 'The pupils' ability to mime gave them an advantage straightway and they were highly amused at the efforts of the adults, some of whom were very talented. The forming of companies from a wide variety of jobs… was successful,

imaginative and amusing too. I had surprisingly underestimated the intelligence of the pupils in this; they were splendid and enjoyed working with the employers enormously, as their letters of thanks afterwards showed.'

The mimes were followed by mock interviews, as Gillian explained:

> 'Most employers and students had two interviews each and in most cases there was a noticeable ease in tension and improvement in communication the second time round. The employers were almost as nervous as the students…
>
> 'We conducted the debriefing in the staff room as we felt the students would feel comfortable there. Exchanges were warm and relaxed. I was impressed again by the speed and grace of the interpreters… Everyone felt it had been a splendid event …The representative from British Gas said that the experience had had a tremendous impact on him and that he was determined to take back issues for consideration to Senior Management and Training Personnel. Another idea for follow up was expressed by one of the representatives from the Hairdressing Training Associates. She was going to learn sign language.'

CHAPTER ELEVEN

The Birth of the East London Compact 1985-7

Major companies were now beginning to take notice of the work the DISCOs were doing and offered support. Gillian Woodward had mentioned the involvement of British Telecom, British Gas, the Post Office; British Rail, Whitbread and Sainsbury's in her work with the deaf school. Another key player was British Petroleum.

Chris Marsden became manager of British Petroleum's Education Relations Unit in 1981. He had a background in education, having been deputy head of Beaumont School, in St Albans, an 11-18 comprehensive, from 1977-1980. He was involved with the DTI's Education Initiative and regularly hosted lunch time meetings of people from business and education at the BP Tower in London, which I attended.

In an article entitled 'Bridging the Culture Gap' in *Linking Schools and Industry* [95] Chris said:

'At the heart of education business links lies the need for

---

[95] David Warwicks: *Linking Schools and Industry*; Basil Blackwell Ltd, 1989 p 21-35. The article originally appeared in a BP in-house production in 1988

> two different cultures to understand one another… When two different cultures meet, it is important to recognise the differences. Points of common interest and similarity are often useful starting places... Many school/industry workshops... have started with discussion of the Management Case Studies, where five similar management problems facing a firm and a school are compared…'

Chris believed the long term benefits of the partnership between education and industry, were three fold: a thriving economy, informed citizens and young people better prepared for the adult world, because their confidence and motivation had been increased. As a result of new styles of teaching and learning and an increased understanding of industry, they could develop new capabilities and skills. However, Chris identified a number of barriers to collaboration, including 'bottom line myopia' and being too busy:

> 'Business people will find many reasons or excuses for putting off getting involved with schools. For example, the top of the "barriers" is "fear of school". This is often a problem. For many outsiders, schools appear to be forbidding places; a feeling based on past personal experiences; newspaper stories about "classroom jungles" and, until recently, the absence of a "welcome mat" in

schools.' [96]

Sir Keith Joseph, Secretary of State for Education, had also spoken about the poor communication between schools and industry over the effectiveness of the examination system as a preparation for the world of work. He described it as 'a scrambled message.' [97]

To address these issues, a new body, called the London Education Business Partnership, of which I was a member, had been set up. Richard Martineau, of Whitbread's, another major company with its headquarters in London, had visited America, where he saw such partnerships in action. On his return, he persuaded nine other companies to fund a pilot project through the London Enterprise Agency (LEntA), to see if Sir Keith "scrambled message" could be clarified.

A researcher was appointed to examine the way in which major companies based in London selected young people for employment and the ways in which schools prepare young people for that selection. I was asked to identify the necessarily small number of schools which the project director would visit. Through the Divisional Industry Schools Co-ordinators, I nominated schools which had good links with industry. Four schools were initially chosen in East London, an area of high unemployment. The

---

[96] David Warwicks op cit p 31

[97] In 1986 Sir Keith Joseph introduced the General Certificate of Secondary Education (GCSE) to replace both O levels and CSEs. Grades A-G were awarded according to absolute standards rather than by statistical rules, which measured candidates against other competitors.

number was later increased to six.

I hoped that, through the London Education Business Partnership, we might be able to develop a network of industrial contacts and an information exchange to match and mirror what we had already set up in the ILEA. This would be beneficial to both sides and above all to the pupils entrusted to education by the community.

*   *   *

In schools themselves, there were a number of myths about links with industry. One was that the curriculum was already too crowded and another 'subject' like school-industry links could not be fitted in. There was also anxiety within the careers service that better contacts between schools and businesses would cut out careers officers.[98] I attempted to address these issues in a speech which I made to the Careers Institute on 30th March 1985.

'On Monday of this week, some of you may have seen an interview on Breakfast Television by Frank Bough with one of the directors of Whitbread and a head teacher talking about school industry liaison…Frank Bough asked Richard Martineau[from Whitbread]: "What are you going to leave out of the curriculum?" This question superbly illustrates every misunderstanding that one could possibly have about school industry liaison…It assumes that

---

[98] In 2014, careers professionals are still concerned that they may be marginalised if schools make direct connections with industry.

school industry liaison is an additional subject area which must be squeezed into the curriculum at the expense of something else…and that the industrialist not the educationalist will decide what is to be left out, thereby confirming the worst fears of all teachers about industry.

'In the ILEA we don't see schools-industry liaison as an addition to the curriculum…like an extension built onto a house when the existing rooms become too small and cramped – an extension built at the expense of a garage … which has to be knocked down or else which occupies the open space where children used to play. Rather it is like an additional window providing extra light and air… We believe schools-industry liaison is not an optional extra… taking place after school, like ballet lessons, nor is it something for dimbos. It is an additional resource which helps us to rethink and review our curriculum for all pupils…

'The findings of the LEntA project are still being written up but the interim report, given to the schools and the businesses involved, was that communication between schools and industry was very badly scrambled and the instrument responsible for the interference is the instrument intended to transmit the message – namely the examination system.'

The Hargreaves Report *Improving Secondary Schools* had identified four aspects of achievement. These were academic achievement, the capacity to apply knowledge to solve problems, the ability to work in groups and the persistence to complete a task. Examinations only measured the first of these and, at a time of high unemployment, they became devalued, rather like the pound sterling.

'Employers, who in the past asked for CSEs, now ask for O levels. This devaluation can be carried to absurd lengths, like the notice in a shop selling records in Notting Hill: "Wanted Sales Assistant – only Music Graduates need apply." Employers admit that they recognise the absurdity but also acknowledge that they use examinations as a filter to cut down the hundreds of applications to a reasonable short list.'[99]

Employers and teachers all agreed that some alternative assessment – such as the London Record of Achievement, which took all four aspects of achievement into account - would be preferable, particularly if there was a brief summary for employers.

'Both sides also agree that it is necessary for them to talk to each other, not to cut out the Careers Service which is, as it were, the marriage broker, but to exchange information through a variety of activities such as twinning schools and industry ... seconding teachers to industry and management courses and vice versa, establishing working groups at every level from a school industry steering group ... made up of teachers, local employers and trade

---

[99] The Head Master of Eton, Tony Little, has recently [2014] complained about the 'Victorian' nature of our present examinations.

unionists, to a central partnership between major employers and senior officers of the ILEA.'

'The organisation capable of achieving this exists not in industry but in education, specifically within the ILEA, so often vilified and traduced, but whose achievements I want to celebrate. For the last year I have been responsible for 10 Divisional Industry School Co-ordinators. None of them is trying to introduce a new subject called Industrial Studies. What they offer schools is new methods and new materials to support the existing curriculum...

'Our DISCOs have three client groups. The first and most obvious group is the pupils whose curriculum is enriched, whose horizons are widened, whose achievements other than the academic may be recognised in schools for the first time. The second is the teachers, who develop new materials, new skills, new confidence and often, improved morale. The third is industry itself which learns about the problems and pressures in inner city schools and also something about their achievements.'

* * *

In September 1986 a team from the London Education Business Partnership (LEBP), which included Richard Martineau, and William Stubbs, the ILEA's Chief Education Officer, visited Boston, Massachusetts and attended the Business in the Community Conference on Youth at Work. His Royal Highness the Prince of Wales chaired the Conference which looked at the Boston Compact. There were notable similarities between the economic and educational situation in Boston and East London, so on their return to England, members of the London Education Business Partnership agreed to carry out a feasibility study, to see whether it might be possible to establish a Compact in East London.

I was summoned to see William Stubbs, the Chief Education Officer of the ILEA, in the autumn of 1987. He told me that the ILEA's elected members had agreed to establish a Compact with the LEBP in East London, an area of high unemployment. It would be modelled on the Boston Compact and bring schools and industry together. Bill Stubbs said that with the abolition of the GLC, the ILEA itself was now under threat. He hoped that the East London Compact might counter that. He wanted me to be part of the feasibility group which examined the possibility of setting up the Compact. A leaflet published by ILEA in May 1987 gave this information about the LEBP:

> 'The London Education Business Partnership is a joint venture between the London Enterprise Agency (LEntA) and the Inner London Education Authority (ILEA) providing a permanent link between business and ILEA schools and colleges. LEntA is a consortium of major companies committed to the development of small businesses and urban renewal… Brian Wright is the Chief Executive. The ILEA is responsible for education in 12 Inner London Boroughs and the City of London. 289,000

children attend the schools and more than 5,000,000 attend the colleges, institutes and polytechnics.'

The employers' group was led by John Farrow, Personnel Director of John Laing (Construction) Ltd. Their aim was to have 50 firms engaged in the East London Phase by June/July 1988. There were also representatives from Whitbread and BP, who had been the prime movers. In the education group were head teachers: Mike Bannister, (St Paul's Way); James Craig (George Green's); Mary Metcalf (Haggerston); John Prince (Homerton House) and Brenda Hutton, Principal of City and East London College.

The Principal Careers Officer, Pat Smith, and 'three ILEA officers' were also involved. The first two were Edward Cassidy, a retired Education Officer, always known as Cassidy, who reported directly to Bill Stubbs, and Desmond Nuttall, the brilliant director of ILEA's Research and Statistics Branch, who was to analyse the impact the Compact had on pupils and schools. I was the third.

Cassidy and I usually travelled by underground from County Hall to the Barbican, from which we could walk to Chiswell Street, the Head Offices of Whitbread. Desmond Nuttall always went by taxi, something which I, as a mere inspector, was never allowed to do, except when I broke my arm and was unable to drive. Desmond often rang up to offer us a lift. Our conversations were not about work or the project but about his family, playing tennis and opera.

The purpose of our meetings was to draw up an agreement – a Compact - between employers in Docklands and local schools and colleges in Tower Hamlets and Hackney. The school heads, Richard Martineau, Desmond Nuttall and I met to identify measurable goals for both schools and industry over lunch in the beautiful cellars of Chiswell Street. They had once stored barrels, I imagine, but they made a wonderful setting for our meetings. The hospitality provided by Whitbread was generous.[100] The atmosphere at these meetings was electric. We knew we were breaking new ground.

The Compact had two aims, one was to improve the educational achievement and motivation of young people, the other was to persuade employers to commit to a potential priority hiring of local school and college leavers. Tower Hamlets and Hackney were among the most deprived areas in London and indeed the country. While the London average of unemployment was 11.5%, in Tower Hamlets it was 25%. School leavers, in particular, found it difficult to get jobs. Moreover, school rolls, which were falling in the rest of London, were rising in this area. Therefore the numbers of unemployed young people were likely to increase. Tensions already existed within the community between the various ethnic and racial groups. A potential time bomb was ticking away.

---

[100] Humphrey often declared that my job was 'mostly lunches' - which, as I hope I have shown, was untrue.

The pilot project began with four schools in the summer term of 1987, George Green's, Mulberry, St Paul's Way and Homerton House. They were joined in the second stage by Haggerston and Skinner's Company schools and the City and East London College. Whitbread and Co. Plc seconded Freddie Jarvis, a senior manager, to be the First Compact Director. He was based at the Brewery in Chiswell Street.

Mini-enterprise projects and work experience schemes were already operating in a number of ILEA secondary schools and it was planned to extend them to Compact schools. Teachers were to be offered management courses organised by business companies. The Transition to Working Life Scheme (TWL) with which I had worked in Camden, was adopted by Compact schools and the companies involved agreed to nominate 'Coaches' to work with groups of school children.

The list of schools goals and personal goals for young people which we came up with was, I believe, more extensive than the one used in the Boston Compact. The employers wanted school leavers who were punctual, hardworking, literate and numerate, so the goals we set for 4th and 5th year pupils were as follows:

1. Not less than 85% attendance at morning and afternoon registration sessions for each of the 4th and 5th years;
2. Not less than 90% punctuality at morning and afternoon registration for each of the 4th and 5th

years; not less than 90 % over two years;

3. Satisfactory completion of the two year course in the 4th and 5th years. Completion involves meeting no less than 90% of deadlines for all assignments, including homework.

4. Completing the London Record of Achievement or a record of development relating to the four aspects of achievement i.e. a) the acquisition and use of information; b) the practical application of knowledge; c)personal and social skills including communication skills; d) motivation, commitment and enterprise.

5. Providing evidence of certification or credits gained, including a recognised examination in English, or English as a Second Language, and Mathematics.

6. Satisfactory completion of two weeks' work experience;

7. The intention to continue education either in school or college.

8. Attending a personal, social and health education course, including careers education, and participating in community service.

* * *

The reward for the students was the prospect of priority hiring by the Compact firms, something which was vitally important for all the children in the Compact schools, but particularly for girls and those from ethnic minorities.

New demands were also made on the Compact schools. They were required to offer corresponding commitments to those made by the pupils. They had to achieve 80% attendance for the cohort of 4th & 5th year students; to ensure an average annual rate of not less than 90% punctuality at registration. This meant better systems of registration had to be introduced.

In some cases, the curriculum needed to be changed radically. In order to enable pupils to acquire competence in the four aspects of achievement, different and more active styles of teaching and learning were required. New courses were introduced to ensure that every 4th and 5th year course had appropriate certification, through the Royal Society of Arts Profile or the City & Guilds Certificate or the new General Certificate of Secondary Education, which in 1988 replaced GCE and CSE. GSCE broke new ground because, for the first time, assessment of course work was included, along with the results of the final examination, in the grades awarded.

George Scudamore, the DISCO for Southwark, was seconded by the ILEA as Director for five schools-industry projects. In the Compact, schools/industry forums, business representatives and teachers met to discuss how businesses could assist with curriculum development – though control of the curriculum remained with schools.

If pupils were to continue in education, which was one of the aims of the Compact, there had to be new sixth form provision, both in terms of places and also of a work-related curriculum. Conferences on the Certificate of Pre-Vocational Education (CPVE) were organised to explain the new examination to employers. Developed by City & Guilds, CPVE was intended for young people who had no strong career aspirations. 74% of a student's time was spent on vocational studies, including work experience. The additional 25% could be used for studying a GSCE or for work experience. CPVE students took part in experiential learning, had access to counselling and were involved in formative and summative profiling. [101]

The Technical and Vocational Initiative, (TVEI) was also launched in 1983, by David Young, then head of the Manpower Services Commission, by-passing the Department for Education and Science.[102] Initially, TVEI was generously funded and during the period 1983-87, many local education authorities, including the ILEA adopted and managed TVEI, which offered young people a broad based curriculum, linked to technical and vocational opportunities and using nationally recognised assessment. All students were expected to go out on work-experience before 16.

---

[101] Immensely popular, initially, the numbers taking up CPVE declined after 1990.

[102] After 1979, he became Secretary of State for Employment

TVEI also led to the growth of courses related to business and industry.

Cathy Avent, Mick Shew, George Scudamore,Peter Holdsworth, Jenny Edwards, Kevin Crompton, Barbara Carter, Anne Taylor, Robert Powell, Michael Joyce

Back Row L-R   Ann Weaver, Margaret Little, Marjorie Wild, Kay Trotter, Vanessa James, Mick Shew, Gill Woodward, George Scudamore

Careers teachers Pat Usher, Marjorie Wild, Anne Taylor, Margaret Ball, Peter Hulse, Angela Meehan, Jacqui Macdonald and others

Kay Trotter & Peter Holdsworth & Careers Teachers

...

Jill Key, Peter Holdsworth, Pat Usher,Marjorie Wild, Anne Taylor

Peter Holdsworth, Vanessa James, Glennys Hughes Jenkins, Anne Taylor

Sean Lawlor , DISCO for Hackney
Farquhar McKay, DISCO for Tower Hamlets.

Farquhar McKay & Sean Lawlor, DISCOs
Trilby Lawlor, Julia Fiehn & Andy Miller, SCIP central team

CHAPTER TWELVE

The Midwives of the Compact 1987-1990

In the first few years of their existence, the DISCOs, profoundly influenced by SCIP's methods of working, were able to select their own projects and work intensively with a small number of schools, in order to effect change. As I have tried to show, their choices were affected by the nature of the economy in their own division, by their own personal interests and their preferred methods of working. My own role, as Inspector for school-industry links, had been to support them and to publicise what they were doing, not to make them into carbon copies of each other. I enjoyed the diversity of their practice and learnt a lot from them.

The advent of the Compact limited this freedom. Their job descriptions were changed, in order to ensure they focussed on work with Compact schools. Fortunately, they proved flexible and inventive enough to operate within these new constraints, while continuing to adhere to the SCIP philosophy.

The arrival of Compact also made huge demands on the work-experience co-ordinators. The first SCIP coordinator in Lambeth, Hilary Street, had a work experience co-ordinator, Peter Foster, but this was not true for every DISCO. In Camden, for instance, there wasn't one, so it had fallen to me to find work experience placements and persuade schools to share them.

In the Autumn of 1987, there were three work experience co-ordinators in the ILEA: Jeffrey Gordon, in Islington; Joyce Bloom, in Hackney, and Bob Satti in Tower Hamlets. Bob had left by the following year. As the Compacts multiplied, more work experience co-ordinators were appointed but often, because the ILEA was no longer so generously funded, had to work in more than one division. This was an issue raised during an HMI inspection of the South East London Compact, where the work experience co-ordinator had to work across four divisions.[103]

In their article *Inside the London Compact,*[104] Sean Lawlor and Farquhar McKay, the DISCOs for Tower Hamlets and Hackney, respectively, described their new roles. They were responsible for promoting curriculum development, running in-service training and maintaining clear communications. Other members of the project team included a work experience co-ordinator, to find the placements, a careers co-ordinator, to offer counselling and guidance, and two business partners responsible for mock interviews and mini-enterprise.

> 'The project leaders work closely with Compact teams in schools and the [local] College. Each institution has

---

[103] See below p 237
[104] S. Lawlor & F McKay *Inside the East London Compact* in *Linking Schools and Industry,* ed. David Warwicks, Blackwell Education 1989

designated a senior member of staff…to lead these teams which include the careers teacher, teachers with pastoral responsibility and the school careers officer. The teams devise and implement strategies for monitoring and supporting students in achieving their goals, and they plan school/college focussed activities.

'Curricular impact: the East London Compact now has a very high profile in Hackney and Tower Hamlets and has produced a marked increase in education / industry activity. In particular, contacts with Compact Companies have supported developments in four major areas: secondment; work experience; job-seeking skills; the London Record of Achievement.

'Secondment … has been a powerful means of promoting change in attitudes (within both industry and education), in the school curriculum, and in the organisation of schools. Secondments involve teachers into industry (and) employers into schools. In the first two years of the Compact over 100 teachers have been seconded to industry. The DISCOs organise a programme that includes:- helping institutions to clarify their objectives; identifying hosts from industry; briefing, monitoring and debriefing the secondments.

'Briefing before secondment helps teachers to clarify their aims and objectives and to develop an action

> plan to introduce innovation following the secondment. Debriefing focuses on dissemination and firming up the action plan. Employers are invited to contribute to these sessions.'[105]

Sean Lawlor and Farquhar McKay produced three manuals to support curriculum change in schools. The first, entitled *Students into Industry*[106] provided activities for staff in schools and colleges to use when planning the curriculum context for work experience. In addition, there were guidelines for students going on placements; exercises preparing students for employers' recruitment procedures; and exercises to enhance the curriculum. This final section was marvellously inventive. The activities suggested included a board game about making choices; a redevelopment game; a photo survey of the local area; a design and marketing exercise and trade union studies.

The other two manuals, equally innovative, dealt with teacher secondment to industry: *Preparation and Placement;* and *Debriefing, Evaluation and Dissemination.* [107] The use of these manuals ensured that the secondments were carefully planned and

---

[105] Op cit p134-136

[106] Farquhar McKay & Sean Lawlor: *Students into Industry*; ed. Helen Long, Framework Press Educational Publishers Ltd. Lancaster 1990

[107] Farquhar McKay & Sean Lawlor *The Staff Development Manual Vol.5* and *Vol.6* eds. Helen Long and Bren Abercrombie; Framework Press Educational Publishers; Lancaster. 1989

tailored to the needs of teachers. The careful evaluation of the experience meant that the benefits were fed back into the curriculum and management structures of the schools. These manuals would be just as relevant today, as they were then.

Secondment was increasingly recognised as an important and creative contribution to East London teachers' professional development. School based activities arising from teacher secondments included:- starting a school-based bank; using company representatives to support work on marketing and distribution; developing mock interviews and improving pupils' job seeking skills; the use of computer software and other resources from industry; curriculum development in geography and A level physics; materials on assessment and appraisal and research into Local (Financial) Management of Schools – something which was just beginning. McKay and Lawlor noted that:

> 'Compact employers have also offered teachers places on their in-house training courses. Teachers have relished the opportunity to work alongside managers from industry. They have been impressed by the task-oriented and problem solving approaches such courses employ and they have readily made links with their own professional practice. Their inter-personal skills, especially in counselling and communications, have been validated by

> the industrialist.' [108]

The traffic was not all one way, however. It was just as important to make employers familiar with schools, as Lawlor and McKay explained:

> 'There is a regular programme of half-day familiarisation visits to schools for Compact employers. These visits play an important role in introducing employers to the schools with which they will be working, but they are only the first of many trips across the threshold. A more intensive appreciation of school life is gained from shadowing a class of pupils, or a head teacher. Every head in East London has been shadowed for periods ranging from a day to a week. Shadowing gives employers an opportunity to appreciate the complex management of running large inner city schools. Employers have been impressed by what they have seen, although bemused by some aspects of school life, e.g.; the procedures by which teachers are appointed; the lack of clerical staff for classroom teachers (and) the difficulty of making and receiving telephone calls.' [109]

*   *   *

Schools were expected to arrange meetings between teachers and parents of 4th and 5th years to discuss their progress. Sometimes, if

---

[108] *Inside the East London Compact* op cit p138
[109] Idem p138-9

the parents didn't speak English, this was difficult. Pupils themselves often had to act as interpreters for their parents. Schools had also to ensure that pupils had access to careers guidance from careers officers, links with the community and links with employers. The fact that it was necessary to make schools sign up to these demands indicates how huge were the organisational changes that they had to make in order to become part of the East London Compact. It was a revolution in schooling.

There was a similar revolution in the kinds of jobs which businesses offered and some of their practices. The LEBP booklet describes the goals which Compact employers had to meet. They had a target of providing 300 jobs for 5th year school leavers in the summer of 1988. They promised to give priority in offers of employment to school leavers from Compact schools. These jobs were to be permanent and to offer induction, access to a training programme and part-time day release, to enable recruits to continue their studies. Businesses also committed themselves to support the development of links between schools and industry across the curriculum.

They promised to ensure an equal opportunities approach for boys and girls in considering school leavers for employment. They agreed to interview students with special needs and to work with the Careers Service to find jobs for them. For students who had failed to get a job after three interviews, they offered to provide, in collaboration with careers teachers and careers officers, a counselling service.

Compact employers also promised to co-operate with requests for work experience, work shadowing and even holiday jobs for pupils; also to organise secondments of teachers to industry and to release business people to shadow teachers.

The London Record of Achievement was an integral part of the Partnership. It complemented the examinations taken by the students and emphasised the human and social skills of pupils. The main purpose of the profile was to give prospective employers full information about the candidates. So a group of employers under the chairmanship of John Dalgleish, personnel director of UB Restaurants, considered the pattern and content of the profile and record, in collaboration with the ILEA project director, Mrs. Jackie Kearns.

* * *

The East London Compact attracted national attention. When the Compact was launched, in County Hall, in 1986, Prince Charles was the guest of honour and made a speech about the work of the LEBP. Inadvertently, HRH's aide, Julia Cleverden, sat in the seat reserved for the Chair of the Authority, Herman Ouseley, which caused some initial consternation, but the speech Prince Charles made was everything we could have hoped for, recognising as it did what an important step the East London Compact was.

Even the Conservative Government, which was generally hostile to ILEA, sat up and noticed what was happening. The

Prime Minister was invited to come to a meeting at LEntA to hear about the East London Compact. As a member of the LEBP, I was also there - the only other woman in the room. Bill Stubbs asked if I would like to meet Mrs. Thatcher but I shook my head.

* * *

HMI's inspection of the East London Phase of Compact took place in the spring of 1988, when the Compact was in its early stages. In the report, there was a suggestion that some schools were not willing participants. David Mallen, who had replaced William Stubbs as Education Officer, was clearly concerned about this and sent me a memo[110] to this effect. On 16 December 1988, I replied:

> 'Thank you for sending me a copy of the HMI report [on the East London Compact]. I was present when HMI reported back to Heads and Inspectors and Compact Directors. I agree that we should be addressing the issues of involvement of all teaching staff and the definition of success.
>
> <u>'Involvement of all teaching staff</u>
>
> 'We are approaching this in two ways. The first is the extension of teacher secondment which HMI identified as a key activity in producing changes in teachers' understanding and practice. Another 40

---

[110] Email was still in the future. We used hand written memos, on self-carbonating paper, to communicate with each other.

teachers will go out on secondment from the East London Compact, with 40 from each of the new compacts in addition. The second is to use the DISCOs, as recommended by HMI, as consultants on implementing the Compact. They have new job descriptions and focus their work almost exclusively on Compact and TVEI Schools.

'The definition of success

'We certainly believe that raising the staying on rate after 16 is just as important as obtaining jobs with training. I have had one seminar this term in County Hall for representatives from East London schools and colleges and sixth form centres to address this question. A small working party, convened by Elizabeth al Qhadi, is meeting and will report back early next term.

'I think it would be helpful to involve Polytechnics and Universities and to make links with existing projects to encourage working class and minority students to raise their aspirations and aim for higher education. Would you like me to

> contact Pauline Perry[111] and others and involve them in discussions?'

*　　　*　　　*

It was my job to respond, on behalf of the ILEA, to the HMI Inspection and present my report to the Elected Members before I sent it off. I still have my draft version. In this, I said that in the initial phase, schools had been selected by Divisional Education Officers (DEOs) and Divisional Inspectors (DIs), who of course knew the schools well. In subsequent stages, however, bids were invited from senior management of schools after consultation with their staff. DIs and DEOs then commented on the suitability of those schools to join. In each Compact, more schools applied to join than could be accommodated at any one time.

HMI also inferred that there were varying degrees of understanding, involvement and commitment to the concept in Compact Schools. I replied that in the initial stages, this was inevitable, particularly as this was:

> 'the first experiment of its kind in the country and was breaking new ground in every way…Its success can to some extent be measured by the fact that the Training Agency has now funded 30 other compacts, nationwide,

[111] Pauline Perry, former Chief HMI, became Vice Chancellor of the South Bank Polytechnic in 1986. In 1991 she was created Baroness Perry of Southwark and sits on the Conservative benches.

> including three others in London.'[112]

As the Compacts developed and expanded, there were opportunities for greater numbers of staff to become involved and to feel a sense of ownership. In-service training was provided for teachers on professional training days by DISCOS and work-experience co-ordinators. Over 80 classroom teachers from East London had undertaken a teacher placement in industry. Tutors were involved in monitoring attendance and punctuality of their pupils and helping them complete the London Record of Achievement. The procedures used were evaluated by Desmond Nuttall and the ILEA Research and Statistics Branch. Compact employers also visited schools and shadowed head teachers. They talked with staff about their selection tests for employment, took part in mock interviews and other industry related activities and attended in-service training. I acknowledged that:

> 'The introduction of the Compact does make administrative and curriculum demands on staff. In recognition of this, a special allocation has been made available to schools from Compact funds for additional teaching and administrative support. The Compact handbook codifies good practice and sets out in some detail how Compacts can be managed in school.'

---

[112]My response on ILEA'S behalf to HMI's Report on the East London Compact.

Compact also made additional demands on the DISCOs.

> 'Timetables and action plans for work experience have been drawn up for the whole year by the DISCOs and work experience co-ordinators for all Compact schools. This ensures that schools are collaborating and sharing resources, such as work experience placements, instead of competing for them. As a result, approximately 1,500 pupils have been placed on work experience in East London alone. These forward plans... also enabled teachers from different Compact Schools to meet and share good practice.'

* * *

Setting up the East London Compact was not the end but the beginning of a process which eventually included schools right across the Authority. A working party was set up to explore the ways in which pupils with special educational needs in mainstream schools as well as those in special schools could participate in Compact. It made recommendations about liaison with employers and colleges of further education.

A second working party considered implications for sixth forms of the increased number of pupils staying on after 16 and the possibility of certain courses being designated 'Compact Courses', requiring students to achieve goals of punctuality, attendance, work experience and course completion. A third working party was set up to survey existing schemes which linked Authority's schools with institutions of Higher Education, to give young people from Inner London better access and perhaps even sponsorship from Compact Firms.

*   *   *

The impact made by the Compact on the individual pupils and teachers in the schools was huge, as two items from the Careers Education and Guidance Advisory Team (CEGAT) Newsletter in the spring of 1989 demonstrate. Patrick Usher, who edited the Newsletter reported:

> 'During the first year of its operation the Compact has achieved considerable success:
>
> *1200 students went out on work experience;
>
> *over 40 teachers spent a week or more in industry;
>
> *employers participated in parents' evenings, careers activities and visits to schools;
>
> *the London Record of Achievement is being rapidly introduced to Compact schools; *the Careers Service has worked closely with the Compact to promote Compact opportunities and ensure good quality jobs;
>
> *nearly 300 jobs were offered to [pupils from] Compact schools;
>
> *a programme of mock interviews was organised by British Telecom;
>
> *students who achieved 100% attendance were awarded

> wrist watches as prizes from Compact employers.
>
> 'The pioneering work, done in the East London Compact, set the agenda for the government's programme to establish 30 Compacts across the country. Plans for this year include: the expansion of the work experience programme; the continuation of teacher secondments to industry, the opportunity for employers to spend some time in schools and colleges, and an increase in the collaboration between employers and schools.'

The Newsletter also included reports on placements by a student and a teacher, both from Haggerston School. Fatima Degia, the student, wrote:

> 'For my work experience I went to the Selfridge hotel. I had to do general office duties like filing and answering the 'phone and also send off for references. I was very nervous when answering the phone and had to deal with people wanting to know about job vacancies. I enjoyed working in the hotel very much and found it a rewarding experience seeing how the hotel industry worked. When we finished our two week work experience, I did not want to leave. At first I was a bit pessimistic about going out to work like an adult, thinking that everything would go wrong; but it didn't and I enjoyed myself very much. I would recommend this placement to anybody.'

Angela Meehan, Head of Careers at Haggerston School spent a

week with Wimpy International. She wrote:

> 'I volunteered to spend a week out of school in industry, because for me it meant bridging the gap between school and industry and acquiring experience and knowledge that could be passed on to students…During the week I was attached to several departments, design, accounts, training, personnel and marketing. I also spent one day in a restaurant.
>
> 'Before I started I had specific aims and objectives for my placement. However, during the week I not only answered those but found out lots more relevant information about the company. I gained insight, knowledge and understanding which proved invaluable when I returned to school.
>
> 'My expertise when giving students advice about job opportunities improved greatly. I personally feel that a barrier had been broken down, enlightening both the employer and myself. Close contacts such as teacher secondments to industry lead to excellent opportunities for curriculum development.
>
> 'Through the contacts that I made whilst on secondment, I have been able to enhance the relevance of my careers teaching e.g. adults rather than teachers taking part in careers simulations. I think that the opportunity for teachers to spend time in industry is extremely valuable and

> I look forward to more of my colleagues being able to participate in this programme.' [113]

[113] CEGAT newsletter: Spring 1988

CHAPTER THIRTEEN

The Year of the Hurricane 1987

On the night of 15-16 October, the Great Storm[114], a violent extra-tropical cyclone, blew up. The day's weather forecaster, Michael Fish, had not warned us to expect trouble. In South East England, gusts of 70 knots or 81 miles were recorded for three or four hours at a time. The damage caused suggested that there had been tornadoes. Greater London was badly hit.

We lay in bed that night, listening to the wind howling round the house, wondering whether the roof would stay on.

I was due to make a disciplinary visit next morning, to a careers teacher, who was not doing his job properly, but when I looked out of my front door and saw the street littered with large branches, I realised how difficult it would be to drive anywhere. I decided that the sensible option was to work from home that day. I rang the school and rearranged my visit.

It was only when we took our walk on Wimbledon Common that weekend, and saw all the huge, fallen trees, lying

---

[114] Technically, it was a storm rather than a hurricane, though the winds reached hurricane speed.

across the greens and paths that we realised how much the landscape had changed.

*　　　　*　　　　*

1987 was a turbulent year- not just meteorologically- though it began quietly enough. In February 1987, the DISCOs, for whom I was responsible, ganged up on me, insisting that I should go on the consultancy course, which they had all taken. It was run by British Gas personnel in Kingston on Hull from 2nd to 6th February 1987. Originally developed for their own managers, British Gas then offered it to various other groups. It cost £160 and lasted a week.

The course was certainly worth attending, challenging as it did commonly practised forms of consultancy, when experts simply told those who hired them what to do. We worked in small groups and modelled a range of different styles of consultancy, from the didactic at one extreme to something close to counselling at the other. In the middle, was a consultancy based on asking people questions about what they wanted and building on their answers.

As usual, when I was involved in any form of role play, I found myself going over the top. In one session, I used a counselling mode. When my 'client' began pouring out her life story, I realised my mistake. I had to disengage, carefully and without damaging her. That in itself was a useful lesson in what not to do. I was grateful to the organisers for developing my negotiating skills, which were to be needed over the coming months in ways I could not have imagined.

*   *   *

On Friday, March 27th 1987, I celebrated my 50th birthday. Several friends met in the Careers Education and Resources Centre (CERC) for a cup of tea and a piece of cake, baked, I think, by Kay Trotter, the advisory teacher for schools, who had replaced Avril Hill. I still have the card, signed by Kay, by Pam, our secretary, Yvonne Beecham, the social sciences inspector, Tony, the centre's media resources officer, (MRO), Henry, a careers teacher, who had dropped in to see us, and my Inspectorate colleague, David Chambers, who wrote *'Very best wishes for the second half of your life,'* in his minute handwriting, which I needed a magnifying glass to read.

David was looking weary and sat hunched over his tin of tobacco as he rolled and smoked his homemade cigarettes. He and I were both due to take part in a joint inspection of the Certificate of Pre-Vocational Education (CPVE) course at Haverstock School and Kingsway Princeton College in Camden in the following week.

As I left for home, at the end of the afternoon, I said: 'See you on Monday, David.'

He looked up, smiled and waved his hand.

I didn't guess what the circumstances of our meeting would be. According to my diary, I was at Haverstock on the morning of Monday, 30th March when I got a 'phone call to say that David had collapsed in Kingsway Princeton College and had been taken to St Bartholomew's Hospital. I dropped everything and went straight there.

David was in the Intensive Care Unit. His wife and sons were sitting in silent shock in the waiting room outside. They said the doctors had told them that David had an aneurysm in the brain. It could have happened at any time.

I went into the ICU. There was subdued lighting and a sound like heavy, regular sighing as the ventilator operated. David, a vast colossus of a man, was lying there as if asleep. I sat with his family for a while. It was difficult to know what to say to them, except to tell them how much David had been loved and valued by his colleagues and by teachers all over the ILEA and how desolate his collapse made us feel.

Three days later, his doctors took the decision to turn off the ventilator because it had become clear the brain stem was dead. David's funeral was held in St Albans, where he lived. Many of his colleagues attended the service, as I did.

* * *

Dr Hargreaves, the ILEA's Chief Inspector, summoned me to his office and told me that I was now the Acting Staff Inspector, for careers education and guidance. I had expected this, but as the full reality of the situation dawned on me, I felt like Atlas bowing under the weight of the globe. How was I going to cope?

'I shall need some more inspectors,' I said.

'You can have one.'

I nerved myself to say: 'Under Cathy Avent, the full complement was three inspectors.' She had survived, whereas David Chambers, who only had me, did not.

'That was in the old days, before the ILEA was rate-capped,' Dr Hargreaves said. 'I'd never get two inspectors past the Members now. And it will take time, to get their approval, to advertise the post and set up the interview. Six months at the very least.'

As I stumbled out into the corridor, I wondered how on earth I was going to cope? I usually did the drive home from County Hall on auto-pilot but there was a moment I always looked forward to – when the spire of St Mary's Church, Wimbledon, was silhouetted against the sunset. At this point, I often started to hum '*Westering Home*' to myself, knowing that I would be in Oakwood Road, in 20 minutes.

That day, I didn't sing. I was terrified by the enormity of the task I had been given. I alone was responsible for the quality of careers education and guidance in the second largest Local Education Authority in the Country. As if that were not enough, I also had oversight of all the school-education links provided by the DISCOS which were central to the London Compacts. David Chambers had buckled under the strain. Would I do the same?

Apart from the terrible shock and bitter personal loss felt by all of us involved in careers education, David Chambers' death left a serious professional void in the team. Cathy Avent had an encyclopaedic knowledge of careers education provision in the ILEA, developed during the ten years when she was the sole inspector for careers education and guidance within the Authority. Even when Alan Hunwicks and David Chambers were appointed to her team, she maintained an overview and retained responsibility for certain schools and acted as a trouble shooter when problems arose. When Cathy Avent retired in 1984, David's association with her and with Alan Hunwicks[115] enabled him to provide much needed continuity. Now, all that had gone.

David and I had divided the Authority between us, with David taking responsibility for the five eastern divisions, while I took the five western ones. Between us we covered all the secondary schools and F.E colleges and special schools. This geographical split had certain advantages. David and I became familiar with 'our' schools and colleges; we knew the heads and principals and liaised regularly with divisional inspectors or general inspectors for secondary schools. These meetings became formalised into bi-annual reviews of the work of careers departments. They were often attended by the divisional careers officer and the divisional industry schools co-ordinator. In this way, David and I developed a detailed knowledge of careers work and schools-industry liaison within our own areas.

---

[115] The inspector I had replaced.

The major disadvantage of the geographical divide only became apparent with David Chambers' untimely death. I was now the single inspector for careers education and far from having an overview, such as Cathy had, the eastern half of the ILEA was as unknown to me as the dark side of the moon.

To make matters worse, the secondments of Andrew Buchanan, the JIIG-CAL co-ordinator and Avril Hill, the advisory teacher for careers education in schools, had ended in December 1986, three months before David died. Their successors, Patrick Usher, Kay Trotter, and Judy Early, the FE Advisory Teacher, only started work at the beginning of 1987. This meant I was the only surviving member of the original careers and guidance advisory team.

The oral tradition which, under Cathy Avent, had been the great stay of the team, was now stretched to breaking point. True, in the files at County Hall were copies of the letters written by the inspectors after their visits. Those written by Cathy were masterpieces of wit and wisdom, which gave greater delight to their recipients than the usual run of inspectors' correspondence. However, precisely because she knew the schools so well and had almost total recall, she had no need to do an analysis of standards, practices and resources, across the ILEA.

Without Cathy's encyclopaedic knowledge of the Authority's institutions, it was impossible, for a newcomer like myself, to answer questions such as: 'How many schools have no careers teacher? How many ILEA schools provide work experience for all fourth year pupils?' Yet a new Government initiative meant that I might be expected to supply answers to these questions.[116]

However, one of Cathy's lasting legacies was a booklet called *Preparation for Choice* (ILEA 1985). The working party included both Cathy and Pat Smith, ILEA's Principal Careers Officer. Its terms of reference had been 'to examine the provision of careers education and guidance in secondary schools in the ILEA and to make recommendations...' The foreword made clear the ILEA's 'fundamental commitment to equal opportunities'... a central theme which runs throughout the document.[117]

Having looked at the educational context – the emphasis on vocational preparation and the revolution taking place in education and training – *Preparation for Choice* suggested that *all* teachers should recognise their responsibility to relate teaching to the world of work and to support the preparation of young people for the transition beyond school.

It considered the role of the careers department and defined six major areas of responsibility: a) Careers Information; b) Liaison with the Careers Service; c) Careers records; d) Careers education; e) Careers guidance; f) Links with the local community.

---

[116] see below p 207
[117] An Outline of Three Documents p1, CEGAT 1988

Preparation for Choice discussed the role of parents and their potential influence on vocational choice. Further sections dealt with the economic and social contexts that affected the life chances of young people in Inner London; the changing situation for girls and the position of young people from ethnic minority groups.

Finally, it described the relationship between the Careers Service, its role in schools and colleges and the process of careers education and envisaged careers departments and careers officers working in partnership.'[118]

Preparation for Choice then set out 22 recommendations to improve the quality of careers provision in school and to elevate the status of careers teachers and ensure they were adequately trained and resourced. This excellent document was the foundation of everything we did and in the troubled period after David's death, it became our bible.

[118] Ibid p 3

CHAPTER FOURTEEN

Acting Staff Inspector, 1987-88

When I became Acting Staff Inspector in 1987, after David's death, apart from a notebook, in which the names of teachers, who attended our in-service education and training courses (INSET), were recorded by hand, there was no data base we could interrogate. The first real contact list was provided by Andrew Buchanan in 1985, when he put the names of the schools which were JIIG-CAL centres and the teachers who were trained to administer the system, on disk. From there, he moved on to draw up a contact list of all careers teachers and lecturers. Before that, names were held in the memories of inspectors and advisory teachers or scattered through the files.

The need to compile a data base of information about the quality of provision in schools and colleges became clear in the autumn of 1986. Dr Hargreaves required subject inspectors to develop of greater homogeneity of practice by using an *aide memoire*, based on a series of headings, taken from *Keeping the School Under Review* and dealing with *the aims of the department; its management; curriculum planning; learning experiences; pupil assessment and record keeping* and, finally, *relationships beyond the department.*

In response to Dr Hargreaves' request to all Staff Inspectors, David Chambers had drawn up more precise definitions of 'substantial visits' by inspectors, in accordance with Dr Hargreaves' guidelines. These were to last at least half a day but might be more extensive. They were to include lesson observations wherever possible. The inspector's findings were to be reported to the head at the end of the visit and recorded in a letter, which was copied to the general inspector for the institution.

As I agonised over how I was going to organise my workload and pull my shell-shocked colleagues together after David Chamber's death, it occurred to me that collecting information on the quality and extent of careers provision in schools would not only serve the Chief Inspector's purpose but also mine. It would be a common task in which we could all join, advisory teachers and inspectors alike, and it would enable the new members of the Careers Education and Guidance Advisory Team (CEGAT) to bond. The information we gathered would meet Dr Hargreaves' demands, while deepening our own knowledge of the field, and enabling us to plan more effective in-service training. It was a virtuous circle.

In mid-1987, the membership of CEGAT was strengthened by the addition of Marjorie Wild. She had been head teacher of Ensham Girls School, which amalgamated with Streatham Boys. The ILEA was good to displaced heads – 'advisory heads' as they were called. Asked by her Divisional Inspector, Norah Shute, what she wanted to do, Marjorie said she would like to work with me on schools-industry links.

When Norah Shute approached me to see if I would take Marjorie into my team, I almost fell on her neck with gratitude. Initially, I gave Marjorie the Transition to Working Life brief. However, her remit soon became much wider. She took on the role of a careers inspector, during the interval before a new inspector could be appointed, and retained it, when one was appointed, so that our numbers rose to three. Quiet, calm, unassuming, her experience of headship proved to be a wonderful asset and a support to me, personally, and to the team, suffering as we all were from shock and a sense of bereavement.

Peter Holdsworth was appointed to the vacant post of careers inspector in February 1988. He was the last inspector to be appointed, before Kenneth Baker, the Education Secretary, decided to include the abolition of the ILEA in his Education Reform Act (ERA). Peter was well suited for the post. He had been a careers advisory teacher under Cathy Avent and then the DISCO in Greenwich, so he was familiar with the eastern divisions of the ILEA, which were unknown to me. Furthermore, his training with British Gas [119] had developed his consultancy skills and given him an understanding of how teams operated.

---

[119] See above p188

Patrick Usher, the new JIIG-CAL co-ordinator, though appointed by David, did not start his work until after David's death. Before joining CEGAT, Patrick had been the careers teacher at Archbishop Tenison School.[120] Patrick's computer expertise was to prove invaluable, as was Judy Early's knowledge of further education. Kay Trotter was seconded to us in 1987 as an advisory teacher, from Warwick Park School in Peckham, where she had been head of careers. She replaced Avril Hill, and became a stalwart of the team.

CEGAT met every Monday morning to review what each of us had done in the past week and to plan the one ahead. It could be argued that to spend half a day on a team meeting was an indulgence. It was, after all, a tenth of our working week.

I was convinced, however, that these meetings were essential for the personal and professional development of the new team I had to create after David's death. Fortunately, its six members were all experts in their own field. However, apart from Peter Holdsworth and myself, who had both done the British Gas Course, none of the others had any experience of consultancy or facilitation. I sensed we all needed to develop new skills, together with confidence in ourselves and trust in our colleagues. Until we were so grounded, we couldn't support ILEA careers teachers

---

[120] It can be seen on television screens when cricket matches at the Oval are broadcast.

adequately or hold our own with other advisory teachers and inspectors. So we regularly set aside time for training at our meetings.

We all looked forward to Monday mornings, which brought us together with colleagues, whom we might have seen only in passing during the previous week, when we dropped into the Careers Education Resources Centre (CERC) to pick up some papers. From time to time, two of us co-operated in running a training course for new careers teachers and lecturers. We also enjoyed collaborating with the DISCOs and work experience co-ordinators, who were cognate members of our team. In addition, our expertise was increasingly being used as a resource to support the newly formed groups such as TVEI or CPVE, as well as the Compact schools. However, much of the time, CEGAT members were working in isolation across London in schools and colleges, supporting careers teachers and lecturers; persuading heads and principals to give them more time, money and space; suggesting new ways of working, encouraging them to make contacts with industry via the DISCOs.

Usually, we were welcomed as partners and facilitators, but there were times when we had to challenge bad practice in schools and colleges, which was uncomfortable but necessary. There were also occasions when we felt our interventions had been less than helpful. We needed the opportunity to discuss what had happened, to ask for advice, in a supportive[121] atmosphere, to check our own perceptions against those of the rest of the team.

These Monday meetings gave us the opportunity to tell each other what we had been doing, to reflect honestly and openly on our success or failure, to evaluate the experience and plan for the future. Like honey bees, which forage far afield, pollinating the flowers, we collected nectar to bring back to the hive. These gatherings became the highlight of the week, which is not true in every job.

Amazingly, the minutes of a number of our meetings survive. I give extracts from two, which give an idea of how they were conducted and what topics were raised. The first one I have is dated Monday, 5th September 1988. Pat Usher was in the chair; Marjorie Wild was taking the minutes. Judy Early and Peter Holdsworth were present and so was I. The role of chair and the task of taking minutes were rotated each week to give everyone the experience of running a meeting and to emphasise the democratic nature of the group.

The minutes of the previous meeting showed that we had agreed to allocate £1,000 of our budget to Judy's Tape/Slide project, showing how to set up a careers room. This was so successful that the Government Training Agency took it up and

[121] Every single member of CEGAT, I have spoken to recently (2014), used the word 'supportive' to describe the team.

copies were sent to every LEA in the country. Judy provided college–focused in service education and training for careers lecturers and tutors together with guidelines on developing a whole college policy. Among other colleges, she visited S.E. London College and worked with the careers lecturer there, recommending materials, suggesting appropriate in-service training and assisting in a survey of college provision.[122]

Pat Usher promised to send out evaluation forms to those attending our computer and careers training courses and to produce a form to record telephone calls and visits to the Careers Education Resources Centre (CERC) by careers teachers. Our resources centre was used not only by ILEA schools and colleges but teachers and advisers from the Outer London Boroughs and all over the South East of England. As a consequence, Tim Walsh, from the National Economic Development Office (NEDO), asked if we would display the Manpower Services Commission's labour printouts in our resources centre.

I said that I had been involved in the appointment of two new DISCOs. Margaret Little had taken over from Mick Shew, in Islington, who had joined the TVEI team. When Michael Joyce, my successor as DISCO in Camden and Westminster, went to Argentina, he was initially replaced by Julia Fiehn, who had been

[122] Her work is described in a response which I wrote to the HMI Survey (1978) see below p238

an advisory teacher for political education in the ILEA and head of social sciences at Starcross School.[123] After a year she was recruited by the SCIP central team and her place was taken by Iris Goodman.[124]

During our team meeting on 26 September 1988, Frances Magee, an inspector from the equal opportunities team, whose remit was gender issues, joined us to discuss how CEGAT could work more closely with her to develop our equal opportunities perspectives.

I distributed copies of a paper I had written on the work of CEGAT[125] and asked Judy Early to order copies of a document produced jointly by the NACGT and the Institute of Careers Office for CERC. The advisory teachers were reminded they needed to fill out a diary form as well as the inspectors.

We each reported on what we had done in the past week. Peter had been to a meeting in Hackney, in Division 4, with Farquhar McKay, the DISCO, and his Divisional Inspector, to review Farquhar's work. Peter also visited two schools there. Pat Usher went to a special school, worked on preparation for a course for careers teachers and on the CEGAT data base of careers provision in ILEA schools. He also contributed to in-service

---

[123] Now called Elizabeth Garratt Anderson

[124] Sadly, my efforts to contact Margaret Little, Iris Goodman or Ann Weaver, who took over from George Scudamore, have been unsuccessful.

[125] See below the CEGAT Report p227

training for the TVEI team.

Marjorie was involved in meetings in Division 6 in Greenwich with Compact project leaders and had been working on a handbook for teachers. Judy went to Kingsway College where she met trainee careers officers and a representative from Barclays Bank. I attended the London Education Business Partnership advisory committee, visited Ebury Street Teachers' Centre, and two schools in Division 2. I met Pat White, the Principal Careers Officer, and had a briefing session with Margaret Ball, our new advisory teacher for schools, to replace Kay Trotter,[126] who left us for family reasons.

Margaret had taught at Rowan High School in Merton, before coming into the ILEA. She was then head of careers at Norwood Girls School and Islington Sixth Form Centre. We planned Margaret's induction, which included a joint visit with each member of the team. She was also allocated time to familiarise herself with the resources in CERC and to learn about the data base we were compiling. Pat Usher asked for contributions to the next issue of the CERC Newsletter.

We agreed that advisory teachers could respond to requests for school and college visits but they should inform the appropriate inspector for the Division, i.e. Marjorie, Peter or me, who made up

---

[126] Kay later returned and stayed with us until the end of the ILEA – becoming an Acting Inspector

the 'Triad.'[127] I was responsible for schools and colleges in Islington, Camden & Westminster and Kensington & Chelsea, plus Southwark College and the North and West London Compacts. Peter Holdsworth had oversight of schools in Hackney, Southwark, Lewisham and Lambeth as well as the City and East London Colleges and the East London Compact. Marjorie looked after schools in Tower Hamlets, Greenwich, and Wandsworth and the South East London Compact.

We decided to review requests for schools-based in-service training at our next meeting. We discussed dates. Marjorie was to replace me at a training session on 14th October. Judy promised to take Margaret Ball to the course she was running at South London College. I noted sadly that the ILEA Schools Branch was overspent and had little money for supply cover for teachers attending courses. Our own supply cover was discussed and I agreed to look for money from our Economic Awareness account.

---

[127] A triad is a three note chord as well as a Chinese secret society and a US nuclear strategy. We preferred the first definition.

CHAPTER FIFTEEN

Maddeningly Mixed Messages 1987

It was just as well that the Careers Education and Guidance Advisory Team (CEGAT) members bonded closely after the tragedy of David's death, because we were facing a national crisis concerning the entitlement of young people to careers education and guidance and, indeed, its very existence in the National Curriculum.

In the spring of 1987, the Department for Education and Science (DES) and the Department of Employment (DoE) published *Working Together for a Better Future.* Among other things, it detailed the responsibilities of local education authorities (LEAs) for careers education and guidance.

This booklet established the central role of careers education in preparing young people for adult life and expected every school and college to have a policy on careers education. It was aimed at all those who made a vital contribution to this process – parents, school or college governors, head teachers and college principals, teachers, lecturers, employers and trade unionists. Its format consisted of responses to a number of key questions which were: What is it all about? Who to turn to? How can the efforts of staff in schools, the careers service, admissions tutors and YTS managing agents be pulled together?

Working Together also dealt with special schools, colleges, ethnic minorities and the role of the careers service and asked LEAs to review their careers policy. Accompanying this document was a questionnaire, addressed to every LEA in England and Wales, asking about levels of support for careers education and guidance.'[128]

The publication of *Working Together* by the DES and DoE, appeared to endorse everything that the Principal Careers Officer, Mrs. Pat Smith, and I were aiming for within the ILEA. We cheered when we read the declaration in *Working Together* that careers education, information and guidance should be right at the centre of the curriculum, because it contributed an essential element of the personal and social development of all pupils and was important from the primary stage onwards.

Its recommendations or 'cardinal points' chimed so exactly with the advice we gave to schools that we could have written it ourselves. These included: someone in the school with a clear responsibility for careers work; appropriate resources of time, support and accommodation; training (perhaps alongside careers officers) provided for careers teachers; the careers teacher playing a full part in the development of the school's curriculum.

---

[128] CEGAT database Report p2

Here, at long last, we believed was support from the Government for vital work with young people. We felt that careers education and guidance, the Cinderella of the curriculum, had finally received an invitation to the ball. However, our euphoria did not last long.

* * *

Three months later, in July 1987, Kenneth Baker, the Secretary of State for Education and Science, published another consultation document, *The National Curriculum 5-16.* [129] Although the consultation document did say the school curriculum should 'develop the potential of all pupils and equip them for the responsibilities of citizenship and for the challenges of employment in tomorrow's world,' careers education was not included in the list of curriculum subjects, either as a 'core' subject like mathematics, English and science or a 'foundation' subject, like history, geography and foreign languages.

In addition, in May 1988, in a speech to a conference on work experience, organised by the Institute of Personnel and Project Trident, the Secretary of State for Education declared that:

> 'with the sharper focus on curricular objectives that the National Curriculum will bring about, I have to say that I doubt that many schools will be able to devote much time to workplace activities unless they contribute explicitly to

[129] DES 1987

curriculum objectives.'[130]

This example, of the right hand of the DSE not knowing what its left hand was doing, came as a devastating blow. For the ILEA Careers Education and Guidance Team, it was like falling through a trap door and finding ourselves in an underground dungeon – an oubliette, in fact. We were not the only people to feel that way.

John Phillips, Head Teacher of Graveney School in Wandsworth, wrote a letter to the *Guardian* on 12 September1987 in which he said there were in the National Curriculum: 'Contradictory messages – a method, which I am told, drives rats mad, and will no doubt do the same for teachers.' He went on to compare Kenneth Baker's National Curriculum with Lord Macaulay's requirements of the Civil Service Entrance examination in the mid-nineteenth century that it should consist of studies 'which have no immediate connection with the business of any profession.'

John Phillips presumed that 'Mr Baker seeks to emulate this position by ensuring that the school curriculum shall be uncluttered by any connection with life or modern society or the needs of employers.' He added that 'it reproduces almost exactly that laid down in 1904 and has no relationship to the next (or last)

---

[130] Andrew Miller, A. G. Watts & Ian Jamieson ; *Rethinking Work Experience :* Falmer Press 1991 p9

20 years.' [131]

SCIP's response to the Consultation Document was that the Education Act should make explicit the importance of schools-industry collaboration to develop industrial and economic awareness in an effective and modern curriculum; to ensure experiential learning in a curriculum context for all students from 5-16; and that careers education and guidance was part of the curriculum for each student.

The NACGT, of which I was a Council member, lobbied the Government, as did the Institute of Careers Officers (ICO). Employers' organisations, such as the CBI and the Engineering Council, insisted on the inclusion of careers education and guidance as one of the so-called 'cross-curricular themes.' Perhaps this had some impact because after the Education Bill had been introduced into Parliament in November, the DES published a booklet, responding to questions and comments.

In his *History of Careers Education in Schools,* David Andrews says:

> 'Careers education was now mentioned as one example of an important theme that would have a key place in the programmes of study for the core and foundation subjects. It further suggested that

---

[131] I am indebted to Gillian Woodward for reminding me of this letter, by sending me a copy of an article she wrote for the Bulletin of Environmental Education (BEE) in November 1987.

> what pupils learnt through this cross-curricular approach could be brought together in the time available outside the National Curriculum.' [132]

* * *

When the Education Reform Act was passed in 1988, careers teachers and officers up and down the country welcomed Section 1 which entitled every pupil in maintained schools to a curriculum which '(a) promotes the spiritual, moral, cultural, mental and physical development of pupils; (b) prepares pupils for the opportunities, responsibilities and experiences of adult life.'

David Andrews noted that HMI picked up this theme in the introduction to its paper on careers education and guidance (HMI/DES 1988):

> 'Following its original booklet on the *Curriculum 5 to 16*, in 1985, HMI published several papers in the Curriculum Matters series on different subject areas. *Curriculum Matters 10* focused on careers education and guidance... The HMI paper set out four aims ...to help pupils:
>
> - To develop knowledge and understanding of themselves and others as individuals;

[132] David Andrews: *The History of Careers Education in Schools,* 2011, Highflyers Publishing Ltd. p28

- To develop knowledge and understanding of the world in which they live and other career opportunities that are available;
- To learn how to make considered choices in relation to anticipated careers and occupations;
- To manage the transitions from school to a full and working life effectively.'[133]

In effect, the HMI paper gave careers teachers and schools-industry and work experience co-ordinators, throughout the country, a ladder, which enabled them to climb out of their oubliette and, battered and bruised though they were, to continue the work they had been doing.

My team offered guidance to bemused ILEA careers teachers in a paper called *Careers Education and Guidance – an Outline of Three Documents*. We knew that they might be fighting battles within their own schools and colleges to retain the place of careers education in the curriculum. To support them in their arguments with management, we decided to focus on the essential elements of pupils' entitlement to careers education and guidance, as outlined in ILEA's 1985 publication *Preparation for Choice* and relate these to *Working Together for a Better Future* (DES/DoE 1987), and to HMI's *Curriculum Matters 10 – Careers Education and Guidance 5-16* (1988.)

---

[133] David Andrews ibid p 29-30

> 'As careers teachers, lecturers, officers and senior management struggle to include this essential element of any curriculum package in an already crowded timetable, it is important that... discussion take place within a context of current education developments. The three documents summarised in this paper are those of most relevance to the careers specialist in Inner London. They set out the ILEA, DES and HMI policy as it relates to the field...'

We said of the HMI publication *Careers Education and Guidance 5-16* that it provided:

> 'a framework within which schools might develop a programme for the teaching and learning of careers education and guidance. Though primarily concerned with schools and students of compulsory school age it is of considerable interest to those involved in careers education in the post 16 sector and further education.'

In addition to restating the traditional creed of careers education and guidance, HMI's publication *Careers Education and Guidance 5-16*, contained two unexpected clauses. First, there was talk about provision of careers education in primary schools. This was not new - many of the DISCOS, like Glennys Hughes Jenkins and Robert Powell had worked in primary schools [134] - but it was,

[134] See the work of Glennys Hughes Jenkins above p139 ff and Robert Powell above p143ff

nonetheless, welcome. Second, the document ended with a discussion of the need to *assess* the learning which had taken place. The importance of careers records was highlighted and the regular up-dating of a personal profile for each pupil.

In *An Outline of Three Documents*, the ILEA team described the significant contribution which schools make in preparing young people for adult life and employment. We identified the specific aims of career education and guidance, in developing skills, attitudes and abilities, which enable young people to be effective in a variety of adult occupations and roles and made direct reference to equal opportunities.

We stated clearly that schools should provide careers education and guidance to all pupils in years three, four and five of secondary school[135]. We listed essential topics and activities, which should be covered, stressing the importance of good organisation, planning and co-ordination. We insisted that all pupils, including those with special educational needs, should have the opportunity for work experience or work related activity before leaving school.

Guidelines for a good relationship between schools and the careers service were set out. We made reference to the contribution of other subjects to careers education – the 'cross-curricular theme.'

---

[135] In today's terms Y3 in secondary schools is now Y9; Y4 is Y10; Y5 is Y11.

The conclusion identified the need to relate careers education and guidance to the development of individual pupils. It stressed the importance of providing careers education and guidance in Years 3-5, in the secondary school and the desirability of work with pupils from the age of five and post 16. Two appendices gave criteria for careers education and guidance, which were useful for evaluating careers programmes. The second provided guidelines for the training of careers teachers and co-ordinators.

HMI's *Careers Education and Guidance 5-16* was a huge encouragement to members of our team, as we said in our *Outline of Three Documents:*

> 'The National Curriculum has not identified careers education and guidance as either a core or foundation subject. However, these three documents [*Preparation for Choice; Working Together* and *Careers Education and Guidance 5-16*] do see the work as having a key role in schools and colleges, initiatives such as TVEI, CPVE, and Compacts have given careers education considerable impetus and the DES (see *Working Together)* has requested that local authorities review policy and practice in this field.'

Two things emerged from our review of these three documents. One was the need for the more systematic review of policy and practice, which CEGAT had already initiated. The other was that we should look at the use of assessment in careers education.

* * *

The National Curriculum Council had been established as an advisory body by the Education Reform Act and given new headquarters in York, beside the River Ouse. A number of people involved in careers education and guidance, including Tony Watts and Bill Law of the National Institute of Careers and Educational Counselling (NICEC) and the officers of the NACGT, of whom I was one, went to York in 1989 to explore the idea of the delivery of careers education and guidance 'across the curriculum,' that is to say as part of foundation subjects like history, geography and economics.

Altogether six booklets in the Curriculum Guidance Series were published by the National Curriculum Council. They were: 1. *A Framework for the Primary Curriculum*; 2. *A Curriculum for All - Special Needs in the National Curriculum;* 3. *The Whole Curriculum;* 4. *Education for Economic and Industrial Understanding*; 5. *Health Education*; 6. *Careers Education and Guidance.*

Careers Education and Guidance, which I worked on, along with others specialists in the field, was a helpful document with an interesting graphic of a circular jigsaw puzzle which showed 'Self' at the centre, with four interlocking aspects: 'Career,' 'Roles,' 'Work' and 'Transition', round the circumference. It gave examples of activities and described possible places within the core and foundation subjects where they might take place, in each of the key stages. It even identified potential attainment targets relating to careers education and guidance, in each key stage.

In Section 6, there was a reference to the major contribution which could be made by the Careers Service, employers and other partners, such as Compact – I'm sure I put that in - Training and Enterprise Councils and School Industry Liaison Officers.

It also identified five different models of delivery, and gave the pluses and minuses for each model:

A. Permeating the whole curriculum;

B. As part of a separately timetabled personal and social education;

C. As a separately timetabled subject;

D. As part of a pastoral,/tutorial subject;

E. Long-block timetabling.

While 'A' was a new idea to many people involved in careers education and guidance, it was something which the DISCOs were already exploring, showing pupils the relevance of almost every curriculum subject to the world of work. However, mapping coverage and ensuring quality could be difficult.

'B' and 'D' were models with which most careers teachers and lecturers were already familiar. Their success or failure depended on the training, expertise and commitment of the PSE staff or tutors, and the quality of materials supplied to them by careers teachers. Model 'E' which usually meant a week in the summer dedicated to a particular activity, was often used by DISCOs to run a mini-enterprise or a simulation. It was fun and a useful addition to careers education but not a substitute for it, in our view.

Our preference was clearly for 'C' - careers education as a separately timetabled subject taught by trained careers teachers. It was also perhaps the most difficult to persuade schools to adopt.

CHAPTER SIXTEEN

The CEGAT Data Base 1988-1990

In the spring term of 1987, Dr Hargreaves demanded that all inspectors should adopt a more rigorous approach to inspection. He asked us to make both qualitative and quantitative evaluations of departments. Subject inspectors were given 10 descriptors and asked to grade the subject departments on a scale of one to four on each descriptor. These were: *general effectiveness; departmental resources; work schemes; differentiation*[136]*; teaching styles; marking; homework, examination results; staff development; lesson observations.* The results of these evaluations were to form the basis of each Staff Inspector's report to the Chief Inspector and were to be included in his annual report in the autumn of 1988. David Chambers died before he could compile such a report. It was left to me to write the first one.

Some older colleagues in the inspectorate, used to a purely pastoral approach, found it difficult, if not impossible, to adapt to the new system. Once, at a meeting of staff inspectors – to which I was now admitted, in my acting capacity - I witnessed Dr

---

[136] Teaching for a range of abilities in mixed ability classes

Hargreaves reduce a long standing staff inspector to tears, because he had failed to comply.

I was horrified. Whatever the man had done - or left undone - I did not think he deserved such public humiliation. When Dr Hargreaves left the room, I asked my senior colleagues whether we should challenge the Chief Inspector. No-one was prepared to do so. Avoiding my eyes, they said that the offending inspector, who had fled at the first opportunity, was 'very naughty' and had consistently refused to obey the Chief Inspector's instructions. This episode, uncomfortable as it was, illustrated what a radical change Dr Hargreaves was making to the ILEA Inspectorate.

Fortunately, Marjorie, Peter and I, had already begun the process of evaluating the quality of careers education and guidance in ILEA schools and colleges, using Dr Hargreaves' ten descriptors and four grades. Our reports were fed into the team's data base, along with the records of visits made by the advisory teachers, Margaret Ball, Pat Usher and Judy Early, who as well as offering advice on good practice to careers teachers, were collecting quantative data on the amount of teaching time and money allocated to careers departments; the range of careers information held in the school and qualifications of careers teachers.

I decided that we should take advantage of Patrick Usher's

computer skills[137] to analyse the information we were gathering, about both the quality and quantity of careers education delivered in ILEA schools and colleges. In 1990, just as the ILEA was disbanding, we finally produced the Careers Education and Guidance Advisory Team (CEGAT) Data Base Report, hereinafter referred to as 'The Report'. It was dedicated to Catherine Avent, who had laid the foundations of careers education and guidance in the ILEA, and to the memory of David Chambers.

> '<u>The Aims of the ILEA Evaluation of Careers Education and Guidance</u>
>
> 'The evaluation of provision for careers education and guidance in ILEA secondary schools was carried out with three separate aims. The first was to respond to the joint publication of the DES and the DoE *Working Together for a Better Future*[138]...The ILEA CEGAT had a second aim in conducting the evaluation and developing a data base of information on careers. With one exception (Anne Taylor) they were all comparatively new. Catherine Avent's retirement in 1984 and David Chambers' tragic death in 1987 left a personal and profession void in the team. The decision to conduct the evaluation of careers education,

---

[137] This experience was useful when Patrick left the ILEA. He went to SIMS the School Management Information Systems and developed a module for Inspecting Schools, which I unknowingly used when I went to Doncaster.
[138] See above p 209

therefore, was taken partly with the intention of avoiding any future hiatus and of informing members of them about existing provision.

> 'In May 1987 there was no suspicion that the days of the ILEA were numbered. CEGAT proposed to carry out the survey and to send the results to the DES and DoE. It then intended to update the data base regularly for its own benefit. However, when the decision was taken to abolish the ILEA, the team felt the evaluation was more and not less essential.
>
> 'The third aim of the evaluation was to present the boroughs with detailed information about careers education and guidance in each school and college when the institutions were handed over to them in 1990.'[139]

Although David Chambers had drawn up an *aide memoire* for careers departments[140] in September 1986, it didn't suit our purposes in the changed situation after his death. As I explained:

> '[His] document was intended for the use of inspectors only and not advisory teachers. Furthermore, it was unsuitable for the collection of statistical information.'[141]

Kay Trotter and I began to experiment with a simple questionnaire

---

[139] CEGAT report p 2
[140] See above p198

[141] CEGAT Report 1990 p6

which could be used by Kay and the other advisory teachers, as well as inspectors, to organise a systematic collection of data on the careers departments throughout the Authority. Our first draft was successful enough to form the basis of discussions by the whole team in May 1987. A new version, designed by Patrick Usher, was tried out in the summer term of 1987.

We showed the questionnaire to Pat White, the Principal Careers Officer, who suggested some amendments to the section on working with careers officers, which were incorporated into the September 1987 edition. A few minor modifications, notably the inclusion of questions about the training of careers teachers and the codification of answers concerning the delivery of careers education and the extent of work experience, were included in the final edition.[142]

The way in which careers education was delivered was one of the most difficult areas to describe. It was like an amoeba, which could adopt various shapes but had a vital central core. We had six codes for the different methods of delivery: timetabled careers lessons (L); involvement in a carousel (C); input into a personal and social education programme (P); via a tutorial programme (T); via a general studies programme in the sixth form (G); as part of a CPVE course (V); no provision (X).

Preparation for Choice (ILEA 1985) suggested that careers

---

[142] The Report p6

teachers should have an incentive allowance parallel to that of the head of geography or history and that in the third, fourth and fifth years 2.5 % of a pupil's time should be spent on careers education. However, we didn't know to what extent this had been implemented.

We also wanted to discover roughly how many hours per year were allocated to careers education and the approximate class size. Unlike the core subjects of English, mathematics, and science or the foundation subjects, such as history and geography, there was no consensus about how much time should be allocated to it or in which year group it should be delivered.

In some schools, careers education began in Year 7, [i.e. the first year in secondary schools] but in the majority there was no input until Year 9, where 13 year old pupils made their choices of GCSE examination subjects. The quality of advice from heads of year and subject teachers also varied. It was not until Year 11, when pupils were deciding whether to stay in the sixth form, or go to college or look for work, that careers officers as well as careers teachers were usually involved.

The questionnaire provided a structured format for visits made by all the team members. Our intention was to administer it to all schools in the Authority. We meant the data we collected to contribute to policy making at an institutional and Authority level and to the national data base assembled in response to *Working Together,* (DES/DoE 1987).

During this period the work load of both the inspectors and advisory teachers was rising sharply as a consequence of our involvement in curriculum developments in Personal and Social Education (PSE), TVEI, Compact, Records of Achievement and the (new) National Curriculum - all of which required in-service training for large numbers of careers teachers and others. This reduced the number of days available for visiting schools.

Crises, including the illness, promotion or departure of a head of department or a change in school management, which might be either more or less sympathetic to careers education, made it necessary to visit some schools and colleges more than once and cancel visits to others, particularly if the department gave no cause for concern. On one or two occasions, although a visit was made, the questionnaire was not completed, perhaps because there was no head of department in post. Nevertheless, by the end, completed questionnaires were available for 124 schools out of the 144 schools and sixth form colleges on the data base.'[143]

In Section 2 of the CEGAT Date Base Report, I wrote:

> 'The evaluation was not undertaken as a piece of academic research... but as part of CEGAT's normal duties of evaluating the work of careers departments across the authority...The original intention of the team was to collect information from the whole cohort of secondary schools

---

[143] CEGAT Database Report p 6

during a two year planned cycle of visits.

'Because of the long time scale, the evaluation was not static but organic. It was less like a snap shot more like a video tape. There were changes in the membership of the team which conducted the evaluation. However, there was a corporate identity among team members, deliberately fostered by joint visits to schools and colleges, careful documentation and regular discussion and analysis of findings. As a result, there was consensus on the nature of good practice which survived the arrival, departure and return of individuals…

'The survey took the form of… both subjective and objective data. The objective data was collected by a questionnaire, administered either by inspectors or advisory teachers during the course of the interview [with the careers teacher]. It was fed back to contributors who were able to correct and update it.

'Subjective data included comments [by inspectors] on the quality of the lessons observed and the nature of school and departmental management. It might be argued that such subjective data collected by evaluators internal to the local authority, are open to gross partiality.

'[The three inspectors] accepted that complete impartiality is impossible for any human being. Nevertheless, they recognised that as inspectors they were entrusted with the

> evaluation of careers education and guidance within the ILEA and that in this area the reputation of the Authority depended upon their professionalism.'[144]

In order to develop our expertise in evaluation, Marjorie, Peter and I made joint visits with each other and with inspectors from other subject disciplines in the ILEA. Where it was possible to make comparisons with the findings of HMI in published reports on careers departments in ILEA schools, we found little divergence of views. So, while we acknowledged that our judgements were subjective, we believed they were broadly acceptable.

In addition to completing the same questionnaire as the advisory teachers used, the three careers inspectors, Marjorie, Peter and I, always observed at least one lesson and made judgements on Dr Hargreaves' scale of 1-4 about the quality of teaching and learning. This was a more sensitive area because judgements were being made on individual performance. We spent a long time discussing whether we should share these with the school?

Our own practice had been evolving over the years between 1987 and 1990. The questionnaire, which Kay and I had designed, was now completed jointly by heads of careers departments or heads of sixth forms and a member of the careers team. Clearly, during this process careers teachers became aware what the likely assessments would be: good, satisfactory,

---

[144] Report pp3-4

inadequate, poor. Often, they welcomed critical assessments because it gave them ammunition to argue with the school's management for more money or time. At the very least, completing the questionnaire was a learning process.

At the end of a visit by an advisory teacher, a copy of the completed questionnaire was left with the school and the original went into the CEGAT files. A written report of the discussion was sent to the head of department and the appropriate careers inspector. In this way, the raw data available to the CEGAT members was open to scrutiny by those with a legitimate interest in it. Mistakes could be checked and eliminated.[145]

Initially, the careers inspectors, Marjorie, Peter and I, used the questionnaires as a way of summarising privately, and somewhat crudely, information which we incorporated in verbal summaries and post-visit letters to head teachers. However, we gradually came to believe that these private evaluations were inconsistent with the way in which we wished to work. Careers education is a discipline which encourages pupils to assess their own strengths and weaknesses and to use that self-assessment as the basis of decision making. Careers teachers were accustomed to negotiate statements of achievements with pupils, and inspectors felt they should be working in the similar way with careers teachers and head teachers.

---

[145] Report p 7

In the end, Marjorie, Peter and I concluded that there was no point in a secret evaluation of various aspects of departmental provision. If it wasn't made explicit, it couldn't improve performance. From the Autumn of 1987 onwards, we therefore developed the practice, of showing teachers the form which evaluated the work of the department at the beginning of the visit and explaining that it would be completed jointly at the end.

It took us longer to decide to share the lesson observation forms with the teacher, because we were making judgements on personal performance. But in the end we decided it was right to do so. The lesson observation form was shown to teachers in advance. At the end of the lesson, we would sit down with the teacher and analyse it jointly, encouraging the teacher to reflect on what had gone well and what had not. The conclusions we recorded on the form and signed by both the teacher and the inspector. A photocopy of the form was given to the teacher and to the head.

We went further than that. We decided we should share with schools and colleges not just our summary judgements but involve them in the whole process. We felt that the arguments for this formative evaluation were exactly the same as those being used for formative assessment of pupil learning by the London Records of Achievement. We therefore made the processes of evaluation explicit to teachers, heads and general inspectors. [146]

---

[146] Report p 4

From this time forward, the questionnaire was sent to the school in advance of a visit by an inspector or a member of the advisory team. Sometimes, it had been filled out before the team member arrived but more commonly the questionnaire was completed during the course of the visit and formed the basis for an in-depth interview and discussion between the careers teacher and the team member.

At the end of a visit by an inspector, the outcomes of that discussion were reported to the head, in the presence of the careers teacher. They were [also] recorded in a letter to the head, to which a completed copy of the questionnaire was attached. Copies of the letter and questionnaire were also sent to the general inspector for the school.

Twenty five years later, looking at the document, I am impressed by the skill and dedication of team members who collected the information under increasing difficult circumstances as the ILEA gradually disintegrated. Careers provision in the overwhelming majority of schools was evaluated and the process we used informed and instructed teachers and heads about the nature of good practice, so that we left them in good running order, for the boroughs to take over. Our visits were like an MOT for careers departments in schools and colleges.

An unexpected result was that CEGAT members also developed their individual skills, of team work and evaluation and inspection, which were to prove useful to them in their future careers.

CHAPTER SEVENTEEN

HMI Inspection in Lewisham 1987

Our data base was also helpful when, in 1987, HMI carried out an inspection of careers education and guidance in Lewisham in conjunction with a Careers Service Inspection. They visited 11 secondary schools and the South East London College.

I confess my heart sank when I saw that HMI had chosen to visit Lewisham, an area of exceptionally high unemployment, as Jill Key had discovered when she was appointed DISCO there. It was also an area entirely unknown to me, personally. However, Peter who was responsible for the Division helped me with my reply on behalf of the Authority to the report, which contained many findings which pleased us.

The summary of the HMI report on the South East London Compact did recognise the huge support given to the project by industry and commerce in London, without which the Compact would not have got off the ground.

> 'The commitment to the development of greater co-operation and understanding between education and industry was established in 1986 when the Inner London

Education Authority (ILEA) and the London Enterprise Agency (LEntA) combined to create the London Education Business Partnership (LEBP). LEntA has the support of nearly 200 major companies and business organisations committed to the development of better relations between business and education. The LEntA Educational Trust has been formed to act as a fund raiser for the Partnership and is a registered charity (No 296521). The Partnership and Trust have the support of the major political parties, the CBI, TUC and the London Chamber of Commerce and Industry.'

The findings concerning careers education and guidance were generally pleasing. I wrote in my reply:

> 'The Authority welcomes the conclusion of HMI that the general level of work in careers education and guidance was considered to be at least satisfactory in most schools and that in four there were noticeably good features. HMI's view that there were two schools with shortcomings accords with the view of the ILEA Careers Education and Guidance Inspectors, who have offered in-service training and support to those schools.
>
> 'The support of heads and senior management for careers education and guidance has always been a critical factor...careers education and guidance is at particular risk at a time of teacher shortages and financial cutbacks. The

> Careers Education and Guidance Advisory Team (CEGAT) has therefore produced policy papers and guidelines for schools and colleges to develop the understanding…that careers education and guidance is part of the entitlement of all pupils… particularly those likely to face discrimination in employment…
>
> 'The Authority welcomes HMI's view that the majority of lessons seen were at least sound and that those in which pupils were challenged to participate actively were generally good. CEGAT, through the DISCOs and its own programme of in-service training, has encouraged the use of active learning and the involvement of those from the world of work.
>
> 'Three of the schools visited by HMI have now joined the South East London Compact and, as part of their commitment … have agreed that all pupils shall have two weeks' work experience in their last year of statutory education. As more schools join the Compact, the programme of work experience will include them. The major brake on the expansion of the programme is that Lewisham shares its work-experience co-ordinator with three other boroughs.'

HMI disapproved strongly – as indeed we did - of one school's practice of putting small numbers of disaffected pupils on five days' work experience for most of the year. I responded that

CEGAT had always made clear that work experience was an educational activity and must be integrated into the curriculum. I pointed out that the Further and Higher Education Colleges Branch of the Authority had issued a handbook on the legal requirements of work experience. Compact work experience co-ordinators had published guidelines for teachers and, together with the DISCOS, provided in-service training for teachers on briefing and debriefing pupils.

HMI judged that seven of the 11 schools were 'sufficiently or well supplied with careers literature and teaching materials.' I mentioned the tape slide programme to show careers teachers how to set up a careers library – which had been taken up by the Training Agency - and referred to CERC, which held copies of published materials and school produced material.

The Careers Service was making 'an important contribution to guidance,' according to HMI, who spoke of the good relationship between the service and schools. This had been fostered, I felt, by the termly meetings between the divisional careers officer, the general inspector secondary and the careers inspector for the division, to review the provision of careers education and guidance. A Careers Association for careers teachers and officers which met each term had been offered funds from our training budget for JIIG-CAL and centrally organised courses.

HMI noted that: 'Many teachers were committed to the

work [but there] is a need for in-service training to help some teachers… provide in-service training for other members of staff.'

This was a sore point with us. Over the past two years, we had been frustrated when our programme of centrally organised training was interrupted and courses were cancelled because of teachers' action, but by November 1987, the action was over and our courses were running once again. Inevitably, there was a backlog.

Our basic training included Stage I, for newly appointed careers teachers. This lasted for two days and the follow up, Stage II, took a single day. We knew from the CEGAT data base that 56% of Lewisham teachers had attended our Stage I course and 14.3% the Stage II course and over half were JIIG-CAL trained. In addition we offered specialised courses for teachers of students who were studying for the Certificate of Prevocational Education; the General Certificate of Secondary Education courses for mature students; A levels, and Higher Education courses.

We also funded a certificate course in Careers Education and Guidance at the Polytechnic of the South Bank. As a result, 25% of careers teachers in Lewisham schools had a diploma in careers obtained by part-time study. This compared favourably with national figures of 4% of careers teachers with a professional qualification.[147]

I was taken aback when HMI reported that the Authority's policy on careers education and guidance was contained in a report of the Schools Sub-Committee dated 1974 – a document I had never seen and which was anyway seriously out of date. I suppose some clerk in County Hall had dug it out of the archives and sent it to HMI, without consulting me.

The Careers Education and Guidance Advisory Team produced policy papers and guidelines for schools and colleges. These were based on the recommendations included in *Preparation for Choice.*[148] HMI described its findings as 'worthy of consideration'. They also noted that most schemes of work in the schools made reference to issues of gender and race. We smiled at that. ILEA had first published a booklet, a report of an ILEA Inspectorate working party entitled *Equal Opportunities for Boys and Girls* in the autumn of 1982. It was a favourite document of ours, suggesting as it did, that the inspectorate should make a firm recommendation that one period a week should be given to careers education in years 3, 4 and 5 and make an initial grant of £1000 to CERC, plus a £250 annual grant to enable CERC to establish a loan collection of videos, cassettes and games for loans to small schools.

---

[147] Figures from a survey carried out by the National Association of Careers and Guidance Teachers in 1987

[148] See above p216

CHAPTER EIGHTEEN

Staff Inspector for Careers Education and Guidance. 1989-1990

I viewed the approach of 1989 with some trepidation. I knew it would bring huge changes. I guessed I might be job-hunting. The society in which we lived was becoming increasingly polarised into rich and poor. So far, Humphrey and I had been fortunate. We had a roof over our heads and two incomes. We had benefitted from tax cuts and salary increases. It was hard not to feel guilty while the numbers of the beggars on the streets of London and the homeless sleeping under Waterloo Bridge and on the Embankment multiplied.

* * *

In 1988, when Dr Hargreaves left the ILEA to become Professor of Education at Cambridge University, he was succeeded as Chief Inspector by the Senior Primary Staff Inspector, Barbara MacGilchrist. With her long experience of the Authority, she was better at handling Elected Members than David Hargreaves, and she insisted that, since I was doing the Staff Inspector's job, I should have the substantive title. It was not exactly a shoe in. I had to apply for the job which I had been doing for two years. I listed some of my varied activities in my application for the post.

I had developed an outline syllabus for use with all models of careers education in the first five years of secondary school and had identified ways of accrediting careers education through the Integrated Humanities, GCSE, and by profiling skills and competences developed by the London Educational Assessment project.

I had worked to establish the London Education Business Partnership, between the ILEA and the London Enterprise Agency. The Partnership supported the Transition to Working Life Project; teacher secondment to industry, the London Record of Achievement and equal access to employment for all ILEA pupils whatever their race, sex or class. I had participated in the Feasibility Project, looking at ways of developing close links between schools and industry in the Docklands, which eventually resulted in the East London Compact.

I helped to found the CPVE steering group, which devised the in-service education and training strategy for pre-vocational education and the mechanics of delivery through the 16-19 co-ordinators and DISCOs. I delivered school-focused in-service training, funded by Government grants and using active learning techniques.

I managed a team of 10 DISCOs, including setting performance objectives; arranging in-service training and an induction programme, and liaising with the Divisional Inspectors.

I attended Careers Service Cabinet meetings with the Principal Careers Officer, Pat Smith and her Assistant Principals and worked to improve collaboration between careers officers and careers teachers. I lectured at the Polytechnic of the South Bank on their careers guidance course and talked to careers teachers in Outer London Boroughs and to the Institute of Careers Officers. I was also a member of the London Regional Committee of the NACGT and ran one Saturday workshop a term.

Barbara MacGilchrist accompanied me to the interview and presented me to elected members. There was no other candidate. They grilled me but seemed more friendly than they had been when I applied for the same post in 1984. Perhaps it was because one of the elected members was the partner of the black deputy head whose complaint against discrimination was upheld? Or it may have been because Barrie Stead mentioned the co-operative workshop? Who knows? Whatever the reason, I was appointed the first and last ILEA Staff Inspector for Careers Education and Guidance.

The CEGAT newsletter for Spring 1989, most beautifully compiled, as always, by Patrick Usher, our computer expert, carried the following brief news item:

'Colleagues may be interested to know that Anne Taylor was successful in her application for the position of Staff Inspector for Careers Education and Guidance – a job that she had been doing very effectively in an acting capacity for the past two years.

I'm sure that you would wish to join her fellow CEGAT members in congratulating her on her appointment and wishing her success in her *new* job.'

* * *

Despite the Compact, linking schools and industry, which spread across the ILEA and was taken up by the Government and rolled across the country; despite the tightening up of ILEA's own inspection procedures, Conservative opposition to the ILEA continued, unabated.

In 1988, Kenneth Baker's Education Reform Bill contained a clause allowing boroughs who wanted to opt out of the ILEA to do so and become education authorities in their own right. Norman Tebbit, the member for Chingford, and Michael Heseltine, the member for Henley, who came from different wings of the Conservative Party, and had absolutely no stake in Inner London, nevertheless united behind an amendment proposing the total abolition of the ILEA. On 4th February 1988, the Government announced it would accept the amendment and abolish the ILEA as part of the Education Reform Act.

Peter Mortimore, former head of the ILEA Research & Statistics department, wrote an article in *The Guardian* on 3 June 2008, entitled 'In Memoriam'. In it, he asked whether the decision to abolish the ILEA 'was intelligent planning or an act of educational vandalism?' He accepted that like many complex bodies the ILEA was far from perfect.

'It could be overly bureaucratic and its politicians tended, perhaps unwisely, to stray into national politics but it was founded on sound principles and committed to the well-being of London's citizens…

'The costs of education in the capital were higher than elsewhere but so were the costs of policing and most other services (and after abolition, the costs increased considerably.) Pupils and students in Inner London performed in examinations much like their urban counterparts elsewhere but had access to an unrivalled array of resources and experiences. Educational television, pioneering computer services, well-stocked libraries, spending on playing fields… tickets to ballet, opera and theatre, and free instrument teaching in schools and Saturday centres were all available. The London Schools Symphony orchestra under the young Simon Rattle, demonstrated the extraordinary levels that could be attained by inner-city pupils. Facilities for pupils with special educational needs were outstanding.

'Much of ILEA's strength stemmed from its interest in innovation. With its economy of scale, the Authority was able to develop a range of ideas many of which were later adopted by authorities all over the UK…such as its adult education services, specialist teachers' centres, joint inspection and advisory teams and the research and statistics branch … influenced developments nationally and internationally. Many of the processes developed by the ILEA were considered unusual at the time. Yet the sophisticated consultation process, parental advisory boards, teachers' and head teachers' panels, expert reports on primary, secondary and special education, sixth form summer schools and the devolution of powers to the then polytechnics and further education colleges have been absorbed into many education systems.'

* * *

For those ILEA employees fortunate enough to be working in schools and colleges, the abolition of the ILEA did not involve any dramatic change. Their day to day business continued as before though they now had to answer to the elected members of one of the 12 Inner London boroughs instead of the ILEA. The boroughs, where there were Compact schools, set up their own Education Business Partnerships, which employed the DISCOs, directly.

While the DISCOs' jobs continued after the abolition of the ILEA, the same was not necessarily true for advisory teachers, inspectors or for heads of teachers' centres, for whom abolition often meant redundancy. The buildings which housed many of the teachers' centres were taken over by the London Residuary Body, which was set up to manage the transfer of property to the new boroughs. 377, Clapham Road, which I imagine was an extremely valuable building, was one of them.

The CERC Newsletter for Spring 1989 recorded our move out of our familiar home: 'The building in Clapham where the Careers Education Resource Centre is located is due to be vacated at the end of this term. '

By the autumn of 1989, Kay Trotter, who had returned to the fold, was reporting in the Newsletter on CERC's new base:

> 'Quite naturally we did not like the prospect of moving from Clapham Road. Although the facilities were cramped, the house had a certain style and atmosphere. We did not seem to notice the endless flights of stairs, and the lack of telephones and desk space. However, our new home on the top floor of Charlotte Sharman School is much more pleasant than we anticipated, especially since we joined our colleagues from the history and social science team and the geography team. The accommodation is in fact an improvement on that of our old home in that it is sited more centrally; the CERC resources are in a larger room; the office space is better; and the hall, tutorial room and kitchen are all on the same level. On cold winter days, when the wind whistles along the corridor, CERC is a quiet and cosy niche. The peace is only disturbed by the sound of the factory hooter heralding break and lunch times when the pupils of Charlotte Sharman School cascade into the playground. As always, we try to ensure that copies of all recent careers publications are on display, as well as

updated editions of regular ones. If you would like advice about resources or would just like to view them, just phone for an appointment.'

* * *

The same edition of the CERC newsletter carried the news that Marjorie Wild was Acting Staff Inspector[149] and Patrick Usher[150] and Kay Trotter[151] were both Acting Inspectors. Peter Holdsworth[152] had joined British Telecom as education liaison manager; Margaret Ball was leaving to become deputy director of Southwark Sixth Form Centre and I had joined the London Borough of Camden as Senior Inspector for student learning and assessment.

As I said in a letter to a friend: 'With great sadness I said goodbye to the ILEA for which I have been working for seven years. It will be disappearing in April 1990 – another victim of Mrs. Thatcher.'

---

149 After the abolition of the ILEA, Marjorie Wild retired to Tonbridge.
150 Patrick Usher moved to Bedford to work for SIMS.
151 Kay went to Merton LEA to work for their Education Business Partnership.
152 Peter Holdsworth initially went to British Gas but later moved to Merton as an Inspector, where he was Kay's boss.

CHAPTER NINETEEN

Transition Skills 1990-1991

Much as I would have liked to stay with CEGAT to the bitter end, I needed a new job. As I hinted earlier, careers inspectors are not as easy to place as science inspectors or mathematicians. There were also some boroughs where I would not have liked to work, for political reasons. Camden, however, had happy memories for me. In 1989, applied for the post of Chief Inspector and was short listed for it but Tom Jupp, a Senior Staff Inspector for further and higher education in the ILEA was appointed. I then asked for an application form for one of the two senior inspectors in Camden, one for staff development and one for student learning and assessment.

My original intention was to apply for the staff development post. After all, I had extensive experience in that area. In my application I wrote: 'I have had responsibility for the professional development of two teams, one consisting of two inspectors and three advisory teachers; the other of 10 divisional industry schools co-ordinators, 5 work experience co-ordinators and a number of individuals working on single projects. In two instances I have been asked by the Chief Inspector to take line management for colleagues who needed support and direction.'[153]

I had made successful bids under TVEI related in-service training (TRIST) and grant related in-service training (GRIST) schemes for funding for in-service courses and teacher secondment to industry and had also helped to prepare the ILEA's bids for TVEI and Compact Funding. I had provided Authority wide in-service training not only in my own subject, but across the curriculum and in all phases of education. Training needs were identified by CEGAT members and evaluated by providers and participants.

However as I compiled the application, I began to change my mind. Copies of both senior inspectors' job descriptions had been sent to me. It is significant that I ticked the list of duties and responsibilities of the inspector for student learning and assessment and not staff development. I wanted a new challenge and the recent work I had done opened a door for me. I was attracted by the opportunity of 'monitoring and advising institutions on their development of systematic assessment, including the National Curriculum, Records of Achievement and record keeping.'

Ever since the introduction of Compact, I had been wrestling with the idea of assessment in careers education. A student's knowledge of history could be assessed by examinations; as could a girl's skills in mathematics and a boy's fluency in

---

[153] One of them, was Mary Harris – I can't remember who the other was.

languages. But careers education was a developmental process and many people believed it was impossible, and perhaps even immoral, to attempt to examine it. I disagreed.

In January 1988, in conjunction with Nick Peacey, advisory teacher for Off Site Units, and Moira Keating, teacher in charge of Hackney Schools' Support Unit, I produced a booklet on careers education for pupils with special needs. It was the outcome of a series of careers in-service training days in 1987 and contained this declaration: 'Certain elements or modules of the careers syllabus are capable of assessment. The Integrated Humanities syllabus [used in some schools] has modules on "People and Work" and "Leisure" which are directly relevant. Sections of the modules on "The Community," "Consumer Affairs" and "Inequality" are also germane. It would be necessary to supplement this course with Transition Skills, e.g. letter writing, filling in forms, making phone calls, going for interviews. These could be profiled by using the Royal Society of Arts Practical Communications profile.'

I had also written an article on *Assessment in Careers Education and Guidance* for the Journal of the National Association of Careers and Guidance Teachers (NACGT). I took as my starting point a quotation from Section VI of *Curriculum Matters 10* (DES 1988): 'Schools need to assess the extent, nature and quality of learning which has occurred in careers education.' I suggested that it was important to address two questions: 'First, is it appropriate to assess careers education and guidance? If so what are the best forms of assessment?'

I acknowledged that: 'For many practitioners the special quality of careers education and guidance arises from the fact that it is a non-examination subject. The agenda is not dictated by an examination board but by the pupils' own needs... As a result, there is a unique relationship between careers practitioners... They fear that any kind of assessment would damage that relationship...

'On the other hand ... teachers who have used... external and internal assessment in careers education for a number of years, argue that this has improved and not diminished the quality of their relationship with their students. They point out that of the four aspects of careers education and guidance, the one that deals with "knowledge and understanding of the world... and the employment and other career opportunities that are available" is eminently assessable. Some schools use the Associated Examining Board's (AEB's) Basic Skills Test on the World of Work to examine pupil's knowledge in this area... Others have taught about the world of work in a module of a core Integrated Humanities programme leading to a Mode 3 GCSE and have linked this with work experience.

'There are also AEB Basic Skills tests in decision making and life skills but teachers who are worried about examining pupils' knowledge of the world of work are even more suspicious of attempts to test other areas of the careers syllabus. They believe that self-assessment, decision making and transition skills are too personal to be measured…

'However, the experience of Certificate of Pre-Vocational Education tutors suggests that the use of profiling in CPVE, which is basically a year-long careers education programme, had not damaged their relationship with their pupils. On the contrary, the discussion of competences is often at the heart of the guidance to students.

'Furthermore, many CPVE tutors believe that the use of the profile assists students in becoming autonomous learners, by helping them to identify their own strengths and weaknesses… and teaches students those skills of self-assessment and decision making which are at the heart of careers education and guidance.'

The whole question of assessment absorbed and intrigued me so much that I took a chance and decided to apply for the post of senior inspector for assessment and student learning in Camden. In my statement, I wrote a section on 'assessment and record keeping':

'Although there has been no tradition of assessment within careers education and the notion has been strongly resisted by many careers teachers, within the last year we have produced assessment schemes in collaboration with the London Record of Achievement team. These are in line with the recently published report of the Records of Achievement National Steering Committee and build on the experience of the East London Compact where the outcomes of education, such as work experience reports, industrial surveys; letters of application; C.V.s and career plans were included in pupils' Records of Achievement.'

'I was a member of the ILEA Inspectorate Committee on assessment, which attempted to reconcile the graded assessment schemes in a number of subject areas and to ensure that the summative assessments were included in the London Record of Achievement. As chair of the inspectorate committee on Personal and Social Education, I organised a number of meetings on assessment for inspectors' own in-service training. We contributed to the debate on standard attainment targets in mathematics and science, outlined in the working party reports. I have also worked with members of my team on proposals for standard targets in careers education.'

Other aspects of the student learning and assessment job which attracted me were 'maintaining an up-to-date knowledge of curriculum matters relating to the learning of students,' and of having 'particular responsibility for monitoring learning and access to the curriculum in relation to equal opportunity policies.'

By the time I had finished writing the application I had convinced myself that I really did want to apply for the post of senior inspector for assessment and student learning and gave that as a heading for my letter of application but I note that in the text I asked to be considered for the other post.

Presumably the mistake was sorted out when I was

interviewed in the Shaw Theatre Complex, where the Education Department was housed for the first few months of its existence, by Peter Mitchell, whom I had first known as Head of Quinton Kynaston School in Division 2 and Tom Jupp. Afterwards Peter wrote a delightful letter to me saying 'we were unanimous in wanting you for the post of Senior Inspector for Student Learning and Assessment.' The job of Senior Inspector for Staff Development was offered to Usha Sahni, who had been head of a primary school in Brent. Usha was a wonderful opposite number.

Camden had also appointed Jill Hoffbrand, who had been Peter's deputy at QK and later Head of Haggerston, one of the East London Compact schools, as head of careers, with oversight of the Careers Office in Camden and also of an advisory teacher for careers.

Cutting the umbilical cord which bound me to the ILEA was complicated, as I explained in a note to Barbara MacGilchrist on 12th May 1989: 'I have discussed with Tom Jupp and Peter Mitchell the possibility of a flexible starting date. On Camden's side, they would like to involve me in the appointment of the rest of the inspectorate team. On the ILEA's part, there are one or two projects which I would like to continue working on, notably the LEBP and the Compacts. In addition, the Camden salary for its two Senior Inspectors is slightly less than I currently earn as an

ILEA Staff Inspector. Alasdair Aston[154] tells me that I can claim detriment [from the London Residuary Body] if I start working after September 1st. I would like to take advantage of this.'

On 9th July, I wrote to Mr. G. L. Peck at Camden's department of Personnel and Management Services: 'I enclose a copy of the contract which I have now signed. I apologise for the delay but... it was necessary to wait until the regulations covering detriment had been published ...it now seems that detriment may apply to those who resign after 4th July... I have indicated that I would like to start to work for Camden on 18th September. This would enable me to carry out certain longstanding commitments at the beginning of the term, including the presentation of two HMI reports to ILEA Members.'

As a leaving gift CEGAT members produced a mock London Record of Achievement for me, which I found amusing and touching:

LONDON RECORD OF ACHIEVEMENT : ANNE TAYLOR

'Careers Education and Guidance Advisory Team

> *'The team's aims are to improve the quality of careers education and guidance in the ILEA's schools and colleges, to encourage links between industry and education, and to*

---

[154] Alasdair was Staff Inspector for English and the official representative of our Trade Union, the National Association of Inspectors and Education Advisers. He was also a considerable poet.

promote initiatives for equal opportunities in race, sex, class and disability.

'Decision Making

'Always involves her colleagues in the decision making process, although her instinctive sense of what would benefit the students is a guiding light.

'Self-Aware

'Self-aware – but too infrequently governed by self-interest.

'Transition skills

'Her commitment and common sense make her a good committee member – her willingness to use persuasive manipulation for a just cause makes her an excellent one!

'Occupational Awareness

'Has been an assiduous collector of occupations and is not finished yet. The force of pupil empowerment can build many empires!

'General Comment

'Her vision of the world is ever optimistic – she sees gold where others see dross. She also has the propensity to suffer fools most *gladly. She will never forgive us for saying so -but she should do well!'*

* * *

I kept a few farewell letters which touched me deeply. One from Marjorie Wild read: 'I remember our meeting at Ensham[155] very clearly and I never guessed then that I would become so involved again or that the next three and a half years would be so enjoyable. Thank you for that and for accepting me into the team. You achieved so much in your time as careers inspector and I am sure you will be equally successful in Camden. It will be a tough year or so but you will get there. Do however take care of yourself.'

Trevor Jaggar, the Senior Staff Inspector, wrote: 'I've been in no doubt about the wisdom of the Authority in appointing you. Your vigour, rigour and good sense have been a great asset to us. You must sometimes wonder at the enormity of the task facing you. But I'm sure that you have had real influence and I hope you feel a sense of satisfaction.'

Chief Inspector Barbara MacGilchrist had been supportive over my transfer to Camden and I thanked her for that. She replied: 'Thank you for your letter and kind comments they were much appreciated… I too feel it has been a privilege working for ILEA and in particular in the Inspectorate. I have a very high regard for you and your work and have been enormously impressed with the high quality of your expertise and commitment. Camden is very lucky to have you.'

---

[155] She was head of Ensham Girls' School which amalgamated with a nearby boys' school

Finally, I had a letter from Barrie Stead, ILEA elected member for Fulham and Vice Chair of the Education Committee. 'I was sorry not to be able to attend your drinks party today. However, I did want to record my personal appreciation of all you have done for young people whilst you have worked with the Authority. We have all enjoyed our contacts with you – your kindness, efficiency and honesty have ensured that – and countless youngsters have benefitted directly and indirectly by your commitment and capability on their behalf, best wishes for your future in Camden. They are very fortunate to have you.'

I have a photograph of a sad little farewell party in County Hall. The ILEA was disintegrating and many people had already left. A once great institution had been dismantled and lay in ruins. An act of vandalism indeed.

CHAPTER TWENTY

Reflections 2015

As I look back in 2015, I ask myself: 'Was it all worth it? Did the courses run by CEGAT for careers teachers and our evaluation of provision improve the lot of young people in the 1980s and 1990s? Did the hard work of the DISCOs in bringing schools and industry together; the development of mini-enterprises, simulations and other active learning methods, pay off? Was the Compact a significant game changer?'

Certainly, curriculum change was facilitated by a number of new developments. David Young used surplus MSC funding to introduce TVEI, with its work related curriculum, in 1983. Two years later, CPVE, which I have described as a year-long careers education course, emerged. In 1987, the replacement of the twin tracks of GCE and CSE by the General Certificate of Secondary Education, which included an element of continuous assessment as well as a final examination, was announced and pupils sat for the first examinations in 1988.[156]

[156] This is now being phased out by the Department of Education.

As a result of these changes and the work of the DISCOs, there was in London, a marked increase in activity-based teaching and learning, which had an impact on the quality of provision of careers education for a generation of young people. Because they had undertaken work experience, work shadowing, work visits and mini-enterprises they were better prepared for employment, self-employment, and unemployment. As Jill Clarke nee Key recently said to me, 'Through SCIP and TVEI, I think we had a significant impact on the curriculum and on pedagogy, and I hope we began to lift the stigma associated with vocational education and qualifications.' [157]

Kenneth Baker's introduction of the National Curriculum in 1987 appeared to put a brake on this drift towards vocational education. However, the HMI document, *Curriculum Matters 10 Careers Education and Guidance,* reaffirmed the need to prepare young people for adult and working life.

Even though some of the innovation was lost with the introduction of the National Curriculum, school-industry work did not end with the demise of the ILEA. On the contrary, in the post ILEA period, links between schools and business were facilitated by the Education Business Partnerships which succeeded the Compacts. Many were staffed by former ILEA employees. Andrew Miller's *Review of 5-14 Education Business Links, and the Final*

---

[157] Email to Anne Dart Taylor 28.10.2014

Evaluation of the London Accord Single Regeneration Programme[158] demonstrates that business support for mini-enterprises, for interviews, and work visits and work experience continued to flourish.

Engagement in schools, which began with talks and visits, moved on to mentoring heads and involvement as governors. Some employers made one to one contacts with pupils as Reading Partners and Number Partners. The great canyon between schools and the world of work, which I talked about when I was a DISCO in Camden and Westminster, had become a narrow ravine which it was possible to cross.

This continuity was achieved despite the fact that it was far easier to manage liaison between schools and business within the ILEA, a single authority covering the 10 central London divisions, than it became after the ILEA was abolished and 12 new LEAs were set up. ILEA's infrastructure, of 10 DISCOs, who acted as brokers between schools and business across Inner London, and who were answerable to the Staff Inspector for Careers Education and Guidance, was leaner and more efficient than the proliferation of EBPs, and other organisations, whose acronyms multiplied like cancer cells, particularly in the Greater London area, after abolition. These unwieldy and top-heavy

---

[158] Andrew Miller A Review of 5-14 Education Business Links in London; Incorporating The Final Evaluation of the London Accord Single Regeneration Budget Programme 1998-2005; Business in the Community; May 2005

structures became increasingly difficult to manage and were replaced by the London Accord, which despite its excellent performance, and over-achievement of targets, came to an end, in 2005, with the withdrawal of government funding.

Some stand-alone EBPs survive to the present day, as was confirmed by a recent[159] conversation I had with a friend, Mrs. Catherine Smith, now head of Bow School of Maths and Computing, in Tower Hamlets. She spoke of her school's business partners, Rothschild's, and the American Bank and said they came into her school to teach the pupils 'financial literacy.'

Cath Smith mentioned that on 9th and 10th May 1912, Bow School had an Ofsted subject survey inspection which focussed on economic, business and enterprise. Teachers were interviewed as were representatives of their business partners in the Tower Hamlets Education Business Partnership. The inspector found that students were aware of the challenges of the current economic climate and the resulting need to excel academically.

> 'Year 9 pupils were able to talk about the risks of debt accumulation through different forms of credit. This resulted from a combination of direct teaching from banks and coverage in citizenship/personal, social, health and economic education (PSHE). The proportion of students leaving school and not entering employment, education or

[159] Telephone conversation with Cath Smith. 25.06.2014

> training is extremely low.'[160]
>
> In Year 10 a wide range of teaching strategies was used.
>
> 'Here students enthusiastically engage with relevant and interesting tasks, for example preparing and delivering a Dragon's Den-type pitch for a school-based business...The economics and business elements of PSHE are delivered by a specialist team whose teaching is supported with good quality resources... it is supported by direct input from business partners.'

The inspector also noticed that:

> 'There are many opportunities for all students to develop enterprise skills through extra-curricula (sic) activities and some students engage in extra activities such as Youth Enterprise.'[161]

I was delighted to learn that the students of Bow School have access to economic education and are learning enterprise skills. However, the present Tower Hamlets EBP differs from that run by Sean Lawlor. Its C.E.O., Mike Tyler, has set up a company limited by guarantee, which is not dependent on the Local Authority. Mike Tyler has benefitted from considerable financial and in-kind support from several large City Companies, including

---

[160] Ofsted 2012-2013 Subject survey inspection programme: economics, business and enterprise: Bow School of Maths and Computing, pp1-2
[161] Op cit p3

Clifford Chance. As a result, the Tower Hamlets EBP is exceptionally well resourced.

I wish that young people in other areas of the country, where EBPs are less well funded or have closed altogether, were equally fortunate. For me, it is the disparity of provision in different parts of the country which is a matter of concern.

SCIP's original vision was to improve both the skill levels of young people and the equality of access to employment for school leavers of all races, classes and sexes, wherever they lived. Certainly, we subscribed to that in Inner London. Looking back, I have no regrets that I spent eight years of my most productive and enjoyable working life, chasing that rainbow.

I hope this monograph may remind politicians and educationalists of what was once achieved and could, with a little encouragement, be revived.

DISCO INDEX

JOSEPH Keith
MP, Secretary of State for Education
p 52, 151
JOYCE Michael
Head of Careers, Hampstead School, DISCO Div.2
p 54, 73, 141, 165, 203
JUPP Tom
Senior Staff Inspector F.E. Colleges, ILEA
Chief Inspector LB Camden
p 249, 255
KEARNS Jackie
Project Director London Record of Achievement
p 176
KEATING Moira
Teacher i/c Support Units, Div 4
p 251
KEY Jill (now CLARKE)
DISCO Div 8
p 32-34, 39, 46, 97, 99-101, 139, 235, 262
KING Hazel
Co-ordinator for Off-site Education, Div2
p 33, 36, 55
LAW Bill
National Association of Careers & Educational Counselling
LAWLOR Sean
DISCO Div 5
p 41, 88, 99, 126, 168, 170-174, 265
LIVINGSTONE Ken
Leader of the Greater London Council
p 80-82
MACGILCHRIST Barbara
Senior Primary Inspector, later Chief Inspector, ILEA
p 241, 243, 255, 258
MAGEE Frances
Inspector for Equal Opportunities - gender

WALLER Priscilla
Camden ITEC
p 54
WALSHE Maureen
Staff Inspector Home Economics
p 107
WATTS Tony
National Institute of Careers and Educational Counselling
WHITE Pat (Patricia)
ILEA Principal Careers Officer
p 78, 205, 225
WILD Marjorie
Head of Ensham School, later Acting Staff Inspector for Careers
p 165-167, 198, 202, 248, 258
WINGATE Tony
Advisory Head for Transition to Working Life
p 55
WOODWARD Gillian
Advisory Teacher for Unemployed School Leavers, DISCO Div 10
p 124, 135, 145, 149, 165
WOOLLEY Carole
Transition to Working Life Co-ordinator Div 2
p 55, 73

46767051R00159

Made in the USA
Charleston, SC
25 September 2015